D0908368

(1985)

J

words,

Dad

THE GIFTS
OF
LIFE AND LOVE

If I But Move a Step

I seek the world
But cannot find its face,
Now I think I see,
But the image changes
If I but move a step.
It changes with every sunbeam,
And every mist of cloud.
Sometimes a mist is born in me,
A sullen mood invades my heart,
The world grows dark,
And anger stalks the streets.
A rising sun within my heart
Can change the scene
And light my day.
The image changes
If I but move a step.

THE GIFTS
OF
LIFE AND LOVE

A Treasury of Inspirations

by

BEN ZION BOKSER

Photographs by Miriam Bokser Caravella

Hebrew Publishing Company

New York

First published 1958
© *Copyright 1958 by Ben Zion Bokser*

Revised edition 1975
© *Copyright 1975 by Ben Zion Bokser*

For Kallia
in gratitude and
for Miriam Ruth and
Boruch Micah
in hope

The meditations which form the substance of this book were written in different times and places. They are inspired by the conviction that human existence, in all its manifoldness, the bitter and the sweet, can best be envisioned as the unfolding of a gift, bestowed and continually renewed by the hand of the Creator.

Some of the material appearing in this book was included in an occasional column which I wrote for the congregational bulletin of The Forest Hills Jewish Center in Forest Hills, New York. It was my good friend, Fred E. Katzner, who prodded me to give the subject more extended treatment and to put it into book form. Mr. Katzner was also helpful with various suggestions which have improved the quality of the book. I express to him my gratefulness.

I also owe a debt of gratitude to the men and women of my congregation among whom it has been my privilege to learn, to serve and to teach for close to a quarter of a century.

If there should be any who will find a better understanding of themselves for having read this book, I shall be well rewarded for its publication.

BEN ZION BOKSER

CONTENTS

1

Contents

2

Contents

3

Contents

4

Contents

5

Contents

6

Contents

7

8

Contents

9

The Gift of Life

THERE is an art in enjoying the blessings of life, and unless we master it, we court disaster. It is a simple art. It consists in realizing that everything we are and everything we have is a gift, ultimately from the Creator, and that every day of our lives the gift is renewed to us. This realization will deepen our joy in possession and it will also lighten our grief in deprivation.

In assessing my own condition, I am often tempted to be dissatisfied. My mind wanders towards what I lack. And if I contrast my poverty with somebody else's affluence, I am tempted to rebel against my destiny.

But my mind is set at peace when I suddenly remember that whatever I have is not, in a final sense, of my own making. Nor is it mine by any right. For what did I bring with me into the world which is my home? I came into it utterly helpless. And the goals towards which I have grown and everything which has been placed in my hands; to have and to cherish, is a gift given me freely, graciously. It was given in love, a love which I could not really earn and for which I can offer little in return. And when I become aware of this, I find a new contentment.

15

This awareness of my blessings, and of their source, prepares me also for their inevitable surrender. For I know that either the things I cherish will not last, or that if they do, I, being mortal, will not always be here to enjoy them. A final separation awaits every relationship, no matter how tender. Someday I shall have to drop every object to which my hands now cling.

These thoughts sadden me, but I can bear them more readily when I remember that the measure of my loss is also the measure of my privilege. Shall I rebel because my roses last so brief a time? Shall I grieve when none blossom in my garden? No! I must rather give thanks for those days I was privileged to enjoy roses, to taste of their beauty and their fragrance.

Each day of my life, my blessings are given to me anew. For the gift given me and for whatever time I am privileged to keep it, I am grateful. And when I am asked to surrender my gift, I shall still know that I was richly blessed. And I shall say: 'Praised be Thou, O Lord my God, that Thou didst grant me the privilege to know the gift of life.'

Thoughts for the New Year

The finger on the clock of time turns inexorably. We are sometimes saddened when we realize that time moves on, that the years are slipping out of our hands, yet these thoughts need not really depress us.

The wisdom of living consists in making the most of what we are given. We cannot weave without threads, but it is our skill with the threads which determines whether we shall fashion a beautiful tapestry or labor without producing anything of use or beauty.

God does not fashion life for us. He does not determine the shape of our dreams, or our accomplishments, but He gives us the threads... He has endowed our hands with energy, our minds with power to reason, our hearts with the power to feel, and He placed us upon the scene of nature abounding in the raw materials with which we can build to our heart's desire.

An artist who has spent his days fashioning a thing of beauty rejoices in his labor when it is done. He does not fret that the days which have passed have made him older. Only empty days, futile days, wasted days, are a tragedy. Only the passing of days such as these is depressing.

How are we using the threads which the Lord has given us? At the New Year we ask this question. It is a disturbing question, because on its answer depends the sum of meaning in our lives.

Wasted threads, badly used threads, show up in the final design, but when we weave with skill, and fashion life into a pattern of harmony and goodness, then our existence becomes permeated with serenity and peace. We can laugh though the days pass and the years go, for then we have given only time in exchange for achievement.

During this season of the year we often recall the Psalmist's prayer: 'O teach us to count our days that we may get us a heart of Wisdom.' No, it does not really mean to count days. Anyone can do that. It is rather a prayer to make the days count. That is indeed the supreme wisdom of living.

A Self-Made Man?

In the orchestration of our existence, our own efforts play only a small part. We live and have our being because we have inherited from successive generations all kinds of assets of body as well as of mind. From the moment we are born, a world we did not make is at our disposal, to furnish as the tools with which we begin shaping our destiny.

Our assets are, however, not only the gifts of man and his world. They are also the gifts of a beneficent Creator. He has enriched the fruits of heredity with all kinds of additional endowments which make us original creations, unique personalities, capable of carrying life into new directions. And it is the Creator Who performs afresh the miracle of birth from the seeds of immortality which He has planted in all His creatures.

What we make of all these gifts is our achievement, but when we sing the saga of our lives, other voices than our own join in to create the mighty harmony.

Let no one claim then that he is a self-made man. No man can make himself, any more than a tree can. Such a claim is born of blindness, and it is the source of conceit and arrogance. A man whose eyes have been opened to the wonder of life knows that his existence is a privilege, a blessing, a gift. And he feels due humility.

A person of understanding will never be arrogant. He will always walk humbly with his God.

Where Does It End?

I look out upon the far horizon. Where does it end? The line drawn by my eye is only imaginary. It will recede as I come near it. Space, like time, is continuous, and there are no sharp interruptions to differentiate one thing from another.

And is it not likewise with my life? I look back into my past. I cannot tell where it began. I am familiar with some of my ancestors, but my life did not begin with them, it stretches far back into time beyond my reckoning. A long line of generations labored to produce me.

The peculiarity of my walk, of my smile, may go back to one, and the bent of my mind to another. The sound of my voice may carry an echo of some unknown benefactor who passed something of himself on to me. The seed that develops in me was planted in a far away past, and as I reap the harvest I know that other hands made it possible.

Equally long is the line of my spiritual ancestors. The love of life, and the sense of kinship I feel for my fellow man is but a simple expression of my spirit, but men achieved it after groping and suffering. The first man who rubbed two stones to produce fire is my ancestor, and so is the first man who discovered the glow of friendship in the clasp of two hands. The men who explored the seas and the mountains and who brought up the hidden riches of the earth are my ancestors. They enriched me with the fruit of their discoveries, as well as with the spirit of their daring.

I am what I am because of the first amoeba which developed into a more complex form, impelled by the divine imperative to grow. A thousand sunsets have shaped my sense of beauty; and a thousand soft voices have taught me to be kind. Waters from a thousand springs have quenched my thirst. I look out upon my world and act in it with all that is mine, with every past experience, and with everything that entered into it.

As I think of the long line stretching far into the past, I also cast my glance forward. The line into the future is just as unbroken. It moves through me into generations yet unborn. And as I think of this I am comforted. For I am a point in that line, and the course of existence travels through me. I have inherited from all the past and I will bequeath to all the future. In the movement of that line lies the secret of immortality and I am a part of it.

The Faucet

The water that runs through the faucet does not originate in it. The faucet is only the last link in a channel through which it flows into my home. My life is like that too.

I conceive thoughts. I am inspired by visions. I commit my energies to tasks of one kind or another. But none of these originate in me. There is a spring out of which wells forth in unending abundance the physical and spiritual power that motivates the universe. We do not initiate the will, the purpose, the direction of the underlying scheme of life on earth, but we are its instruments, who are given some opportunity to cooperate with the world's purpose, and to implement it. My muscle and my brain are the final links in a channel that draws its precious elements from the divine source of all life.

Shall the faucet complain that it can contain only a tiny

quantity of water? Shall I complain that only a tiny portion of life's assets reside in me? The abundance does not have to be in the faucet, nor does it have to be in me. There is an unending fountain from which more will flow, and it will reach me when I am ready for it.

My Life Is Not My Own

'It is my life. I can do with it as I please.' How often have you heard that defiant declaration of independence? Yet, it is based on no more than a half-truth.

It is true that every man has a duty, not to speak of a right, to live by his own lights. No man was meant to be a duplicate of another, or echo someone else's voice. The Creator made each of us a distinctive person, with a mind of his own. Presumably He wanted us to live by it, to justify making us what we are.

Yet, our life is not entirely our own, and we do not have an unqualified right to do what we please. Our parents, our friends, our society too, have all made investments in us, and what we do makes a difference to them! We are obliged to consider whether we are conserving or dissipating their investments.

The greatest investor in our lives is God, Who conferred existence upon us, and Who endowed us with potentialities waiting to be awakened by us to active life. The Creator's work is never without a purpose, so there is then a goal, a commitment to which our lives are charged. A man may refuse to pay his bills, but a record exists. A charge is entered against every name and we are all in duty bound to redeem our outstanding obligations.

'My life is not my own.' It is a trust for which I am

responsible. I have no right to do with it as I please, but I am under an obligation to discharge the terms of the trust.

Towards a Noble Harvest

Youth has been called the spring-time of a man's life. It is an appropriate comparison, as spring is the time when nature mobilizes all her energies for new adventures, and youth is like that too. It is the time when every fibre of one's being is glowing with vitality, and the readiness for bold new tasks. It is the time for the dreams and visions which beckon us.

But spring is not merely the time for adventure; it is also the time of preparation, the time of planting and sowing. In spring the world awakens to make ready for the harvest of tomorrow. Youth also has this task of preparing its strength to bring into the world the ripened fruits of maturity.

Each of us has the capacity to render some service to our fellow man. Be they much or little, distinguished or humble, the good deeds we perform are the fruits which our lives were expected to produce for humanity. But our capacities will remain asleep in our souls unless they are encouraged to develop, for they are the seeds the Lord placed in our beings at birth, and we must prepare the soil for them to germinate and yield the fullness of their promise.

One of the questions which every young person ought to ask himself is: Will I develop sufficiently to yield some precious fruit at the time of my harvest? Am I storing up a fund of knowledge about man and the world to draw upon in later years? Am I imbibing the thoughts of great masters from whom I may find guidance in my own tasks in life? Do I offer my mind the stimulation of diverse ideas, the exhilaration of the uninhibited search for truth? This is how we prepare the garden of our lives so that the precious seeds imbedded there shall germinate and come to fruition.

Barren men whose lives contain no nourishment for the fruit of the human soul are pathetic indeed. They are as pathetic as the barren trees, as the barren earth which can only produce weeds.

O God, do Thou watch over our youth and guide it to make the ways of its spring a prelude to a bounteous harvest.

The Worm and I

What does a worm do for its livelihood? It works without ceasing, tunnelling beneath the surface, keeping the earth from excessive hardening. But where does it get its own nourishment, to maintain its health and to give it energy to carry on its labors?

There is an economy in the rhythms of nature. Each creature has a purpose, each has a job to do and the same hand that placed these creatures on earth and assigned them their duties, also provided for their sustenance. The ant, the sparrow, the worm, and their fellow creatures that inhabit the spaces of the world all share in the same divine plan. Each serves in its own way and each is sustained in its own way.

Because I know that there is such a plan, I am confident in my own destiny. It is improbable that He who provided for the worm did not provide for me. Man is a free agent and he has the privilege of exercising his own judgment in selecting the work by which he serves and is himself sustained. But I depend not on my particular job, nor on the man who makes it available. I am not dependent on my employer, my customer, my client, but on the Lord my God, my true Benefactor, who sustains the whole world with grace and with lovingkindness.

Dig More Deeply

The peanut is one of the humble products in the granary of nature. But in the hands of a scientist such as George Washington Carver, it was revealed to be infinitely rich in all kinds of possibilities. From peanuts he made a dozen beverages, mixed pickles, instant and dry coffee, tan remover, wood filler, paper, ink, shaving cream, linoleum, and synthetic rubber. Things are not always what they seem at first. By exploring beneath the surface we often discover that what we judged of little worth really contains hidden treasures waiting to be claimed by man.

We have often dismissed life as valueless because we did not probe it deeply enough. In our friends, in our children, in ourselves, lie dormant all kinds of strength we little suspect. We need to undertake voyages of discovery to lay bare the hidden continents of life's possibilities. The recent popularization of such hobbies as painting and sculpture, has startled many of us with the revelation of talent among seemingly ungifted people. In emergencies we have all revealed powers of body and mind of which we were seldom aware. We are all richer than we realize.

Who ever imagined what stupendous energies lay stored

up in a single atom of uranium? There are levels of being whose depths we must seek throughout all our lives. He who only lives on the surface enjoys but the outer crust; he who reaches beneath the surface begins to claim his hidden treasures.

Have you ever rebelled because you thought your life was too drab? Dig more deeply. Seek its potentialities. By the alchemy of your probing, your life will often turn from grey to gold.

The Loveliness of a Child

'O to keep the loveliness of a child that fades with the years!' Have you ever been moved by that reflection? I was, on looking at the picture of my daughter when she was two years old. She is now fourteen, and graceful and pretty for her age. But there is a special softness and charm which only a young infant possesses. And this special charm vanishes as the child grows older.

The loveliness of a tender child is part of its armor of life. It was put there by the Almighty to compensate the father and mother for the arduous care which the child requires during those early years. A parent would otherwise be less willing to put up with that tedious round of wakeful nights, of struggling to feed and keep clean and sustain in health this totally helpless creature. The Lord made that infant so lovely, with a skin so soft to the touch, with a smile so captivating, that the parents are enchanted, and the labor of caring for that infant is rendered so sweet.

That infant must grow up, however, and eventually attain independence. He will have to learn to stand on his own feet. The little boy must finally become a man and leave his father and mother and cleave unto his wife so that they become one flesh. The transition sets in early. That loveliness, that special endearing charm begins to fade, so that the grief of separation may be more bearable to the parents.

The boy and the girl will then need other charms—charms to attract a mate with a new kind of love. The Lord provides those charms too in due measure and in due time.

There are instances where parents or children act contrary to the Lord's intentions. Mothers, and fathers too, because their own lives are deficient in other fulfillments will occasionally seek to hold their children and refuse to let them go. They will want to keep the grown son or daughter for themselves, impeding their emergence into the world of adult existence. And there are instances of grown sons and daughters remaining so attached to their parents that they are incapable of the new adjustments for which the time has come.

These are instances of infantilism, of immaturity, of failure to grow up. True growth must be emotional as well as physical.

The Lord has made everything good in its time. That which *in its time* is good, becomes a tragic absurdity when its time is past.

Let us enjoy the loveliness of a child and when that special childhood loveliness begins to fade, let us not grieve, for our child is then moving to a new career, wonderful in its own way—maturity.

Are Marriages Made in Heaven?

'Marriages are made in heaven,' said the grandmother. By this she meant to convey to her sophisticated granddaughter the humbling yet reassuring lesson that the Lord who had given her life would also provide her with a mate.

The young lady smiled. She considered that finding a mate was the end of an active quest. She remembered the more practical wisdom imparted by one of her friends: 'You have to go out to get your man.' Inevitably she reflected on her next date: 'What gown shall I wear? What cosmetics shall I use? How shall I wear my hair?'

She did get her man but not the one with whom she had had that date. It was a man she met at the florist, when both were buying flowers for their mothers on Mothers' Day.

In a mood of self-assessment in which couples in love occasionally indulge, her man once said to her: 'You know, dear, there is something about you for which my deepest self has hungered all through the years. I thank the Lord who made you as you are.'

The young lady mused a while, and said: 'It is only because you are as you are that I could appeal so satisfyingly to your deepest self. I thank the Lord who made you as you are.'

'We were meant for each other,' both exclaimed enthusiastically at the same time.

And then a smile crossed the young lady's face. She suddenly remembered what her grandmother had told her.

Enduring Fire

Young couples occasionally look back with nostalgia on the romantic beginnings of their love. The bonds which now link them to each other are real and deep, yet they remember the earlier exhilaration, when each encounter was an adventure, long anticipated, and long remembered. They sometimes feel as though all the sparkle, all the poetry has gone out of their lives.

Their complaint is in some sense true, but they do not fully understand the meaning of the change which has taken place in their lives. The excitation was a necessary stimulant to courtship. It was necessary to overcome the resistance to the loss of independence, which is in some respects inevitable when two lives are to be merged into one. A tree, in the early stages of its transplantation needs special nurture, and so do young people at the time of the most radical change in their lives.

That stimulant recedes when it has accomplished its purpose. Indeed its persistence might become a hindrance, since these young people whose pursuit of each other has ended with the prize won, now have other things to do. They must begin the prose of everyday life. They must begin to share the rigours of living, to face common tasks, to help each other in their climb towards the new horizons opening in their life together.

The thin kindling wood gives off a brilliant flame, but that flame cannot last, and does not give out warmth. Its function is to ignite the heavy log, which will burn with less sparkle, less glitter, but with the most glowing steadiness. The fire of later years is not as brilliant as the blaze which burned at the beginning but it is firmer, surer, warmer.

Let us not permit the kindling wood to flare up and burn itself out in a beautiful but brief exhibit of flame, without being sure it ignites the thicker log for the more enduring fire.

Boredom

Have you ever been bored? When we have nothing in particular to do, and have time on our hands, a strange unrest seizes us, and we feel our life to be futile and meaningless.

Boredom is not an uncommon human experience. It is a divine judgment against our uncreative life. The Lord placed us in this world for a purpose. We have tasks waiting to be done. In us there is the energy of hand and heart and mind, craving for release, for action. Yet we allow the tasks to remain undone, and our energies to be untapped. Our feeling of boredom is an indication of God's displeasure with what we are making of ourselves. This unrest of the soul calls for no special cure except work, work that will serve someone in the world, work that will give us the most priceless of all joys – the satisfaction of being useful, of being creative.

God has woven many safeguards, for our own well-being, into the fabric of our natures. In the face of peril we are pervaded by an emotion of fear. When our bodies need sustenance, we feel a sensation of hunger. Because the Lord wanted us to live with mates in the family of life, He gave us the sexual urge. These pressures in our nature are the controls the Lord has set upon us to steer us the way He wishes us to go. Boredom is just such a control.

The Lord did not want us to stagnate through idleness. We each have a job we can do, and should do. It may be a rigorous job, and initially it may appear hard, even beyond us. But let us put our hand and heart to it, and if we suffer from any feeling of boredom, it will fade before we know it, as morning mist fades at the oncoming sun.

Weeds

A farmer once sighed after he had finished weeding his garden. His back was bent, the perspiration ran down his face. 'If not for those cursed weeds,' he said to himself, 'gardening would be such a joy. Why God made weeds is really beyond me.'

The farmer mused a little as he contemplated the heap of weeds he had pulled out. Suddenly one of the weeds spoke up. Its face was already pale and wilting, but it mustered enough strength to speak in self-defense.

'You should not speak ill of any of God's creatures.' the little weed said. 'You have given us a bad name and decried our presence in the world. We render you a thousand uses you may not be aware of. We tend your soil when you are not there to cultivate it. We prevent your precious earth from being washed away by the rain. We do not allow it to be carried away by the wind as dust. And do we not justify our existence even in your carefully cultivated garden? Your flowers would never be able to stand the elements, to survive the blowing winds and lashing rains, if we did not toughen them. In their skirmishes with us they gain strength. When you enjoy their splendor, remember that we had a part in their growth.'

The weed made a marked impression, and then although almost exhausted it continued in a peroration: 'The vegetation you cultivate is like the people in your own world. They need some opposition to be toughened for the formidable business of living.'

The weed resumed its silence. The farmer straightened his back as he wiped his brow. A smile of satisfaction came over his face. He looked out on the field that was yet to be weeded, but he knew that weeding would no longer be a disagreeable task.

The Rose Talked Back

The man sweeping the synagogue paused for a moment. He looked at the flowers lying about in disorder. 'What waste!' he said to himself. Those roses had adorned the pulpit at a wedding an hour before. Now all was over and they were waiting to be discarded.

The attendant leaning on his sweeper was lost in thought when suddenly he heard a strange sound. One of the roses replied to him.

'Do you call this a waste?' the flower protested. 'What is life anyway, yours or mine, but a means of service? My mission was to create some fragrance and beauty, and when I have fulfilled it my life has not been wasted. And what greater privilege is there than to adorn a bride's way to her beloved, what greater privilege than to help glorify the moment when a bride and groom seal their faith in each other by entering the covenant of marriage?'

Our little flower paused for a moment to watch the man's face, and then continued her discourse.

'Roses are like people. They live in deeds, not in time.

My glory was but for a brief hour, but you should have seen the joy in the bride's eye. I like to believe that I had something to do with it, by creating a suitable setting for the moment of her supreme happiness. So don't grieve for me. My life has been worthwhile.'

Having spoken her little piece, the rose was once more silent. The attendant, startled from his reverie and a little wiser, pushed the sweeper again and continued with his work.

Is Time a Great Healer?

'Time is a great healer.' You have often heard that, but have you ever paused to think how absurd a statement it is?

Time itself does not act. Only one who has a will, only one who has a mind and purpose of his own, can act. A healer is one who knows what pain is, who loves life and seeks to prolong and improve it. Time is an abstraction, the span of moments or of days within which actions occur. So time itself cannot heal us.

When we say 'time is a great healer' we mean that apparently without man's intervention our bodies and our spirits are mended. This is true. But while man does not intervene, a great doctor, unseen to the human eye, does the work of healing. Our grief gradually recedes, the bruises in our skin disappear, the ache in our hearts gives way. God who formed life endowed it with amazing recuperative powers. The process of recuperation takes time, but the restorer of health is He who is also the giver of life – Almighty God.

God is the great Healer and He heals in time.

Health Is Relative

Have you ever met a perfectly healthy person? I am certain that you have not, because such a person does not exist. Everyone suffers from some deficiency, from some impairment of one organ or another.

And what is true of physical health is also true of mental health. No life is perfectly serene, without some distress, without some grief.

Health is relative. A wholesome person is one who lives with the consciousness of his strength. Morbidity consists in concentrating on our aches and pains. If there be enough energy at our disposal to balance our weakness, then we need not fear, for we then have sufficient strength to meet the commitments of living.

Let us be among those whose lives are determined by their strength rather than by their weakness.

Rust

Have you ever considered the real significance of rust?

Creation goes on day by day. The momentous words, 'Let there be light,' by which God launched the universe, started the process, but it is unfinished. As we master the laws of nature, as we understand the hidden forces at work in our own lives, and with that knowledge fashion a nobler world, we are continuing the work of creation. Among the many aids that God has provided for our work is rust.

Continuous creation involves replacing the old with the new. That which has played its part in the drama of existence must give way, so that the fresh may make its appearance. Rust, like every other form of decay, removes the obsolete from the scene to make room for the new, and without it the world would long have become clogged up with accumulations of junk. The debris of death would have crowded out life. Rust is the sanitation department in God's universe.

Rust has a parallel in human phenomena. Forgetfulness is a kind of rust working on past experience. Because we forget the old we can more readily embrace the new. One shudders to think what would happen if we could not forget, if our minds were forced to carry all our memories in active consciousness.

The human phenomenon which offers the closest parallel to rust is death. One generation dies that a new generation may take its place. A mature person cannot therefore rebel against death. It is the price we must always pay for the emergence of new life. Death and life are only the opposite sides of the same coin. We can't have one without the other.

Death Is Not Extinction

Death is not a total extinction of life; it is like the sculptor's smashing of a clay model. The form is destroyed; but it returns to its raw matter out of which the artist will attempt some new creation.

In the economy of God's universe, there is a conservation of elements. We may disintegrate an atom, but the essence survives in the stupendous energy which has been released. Similarly death cannot destroy the body or the soul. The body returns to the treasury of primordial earth from which all physical life emerges and to which it returns. It decomposes into its constituent elements and continues to be part of the cycle of unending existence. The soul is invisible and it returns to its invisible living source. And if we have lived with any beauty or goodness during the span of our years, then that beauty or goodness has entered the permanent reservoir of life's assets, and it will continue to exist in newer incarnations; our deeds will be an inspiration to other lives.

Even our individuality is not wholly lost. For the seeds of immortality have been planted in us, and out of these seeds spring new life. For the Creator is infinitely resourceful and He employs the same stuff of life in eternally novel ways. Yet in that new life, we live on, for it is flesh of our flesh and spirit of our spirit.

Destruction is a prelude to new creation. It enables the Architect of our existence to wipe clean the slate at intervals and to start over again. The loss of the old is vindicated in the new – in the fairer copy which comes after it.

A Righteous Judge

All life is a gift from the hand of the Creator. It is an ever-recurring miracle which renews the wonder of creation. And when life is withdrawn, we dare not fret, for its withdrawal is a reminder of the privilege we enjoyed during the time we were permitted to keep the gift.

The greatest grief comes to those who regard the world as their very own, for when deprived of something they feel that a great injustice has been committed. Happy are the enlightened who realize that we are here only by the invitation of the divine Host who is the true Master of the universe. A guest is conscious of being privileged by whatever token of recognition he receives from his host, though he knows that whatever is showered on him will be withheld before long. The Lord only takes what He in the first place has given.

The withdrawal of the gift arouses a feeling of gratitude in a sensitive person for whatever time he was privileged to keep it. He will grieve because he misses what he has lost, but he will praise God as a righteous Judge.

Barbara Was Thoughtless

'You forgot something, Barbara. You didn't say "good-night." ' I heard this call ring out across the street one evening. I do not know Barbara, nor the little girl who thus reminded her friend of a lapse from thoughtfulness. The call to Barbara has somehow lingered in my mind, as a symbol of a general failing in modern man.

Barbara presumably enjoyed her friend's hospitality. She had been with her for some time, they had played together; they had lived together. Friendship is a privilege, which Barbara was blessed with. Is it not proper to express a thankfulness for this privilege? How then could she leave her friend without saying a word, not even a good-night?

Is not this thoughtlessness the problem of man generally? We take for granted the love of our parents, their care and devotion, the anxious hours spent by them in seeing us through all kinds of hardship. We take for granted the kindness of our friends and neighbors. We take from the poets and the artists, the scientists and the men of affairs the blessings their genius has brought into the world. We take all of it without pausing to think of how much we owe them.

What, if not a sense of gratitude, is the object of religion? It seeks to awaken in us an awareness of the greatest privilege of all – the privilege of the blessings we receive from God. Most of us also take His blessings without due thought. We breathe the calm, clear air; we watch the stars in their majestic cadences in the sky; we enjoy the fragrance of flowers and the laughter of children; we draw upon the energies of our hands and brains to perform our tasks; we dream and hope; and we create in the image of our dreams and hopes. But we take all as our due, without a word of appreciation. This is why modern man cannot pray. Prayer is our expression of thanks to God for the privilege of living. Most modern people take all life for granted, and they do not bother to say 'thank you.'

Barbara was only thoughtless. But thoughtlessness is one of the greatest failings of character. When you leave your friends, say 'good-night.' When you are the recipient of blessings, whether from God or man, learn to say 'thank you.'

The Constant Giver

The constant giver is not properly appreciated. The very frequency of his gifts causes us to take him for granted. The child who receives a little trinket from his aunt will be profusely thankful, but his mother's unending affection evokes no such enthusiastic response.

We are incapable of being permanently aware of our indebtedness. Our gifts have been too numerous and the work of recounting them all would be too great a burden;

we therefore respond selectively. We only become aware of what we have when our possession of it has become precarious. After days of continual clouds and rain, we love the sunshine, and after days of continual sun, we long for a change, and bless the rain.

The gifts of the constant giver become so much a part of our pattern of life, that we can't imagine life without them, and therefore the privilege of living with them evokes no special emotion. It is only the very rare child who feels the immense gratitude he owes to his father or mother. Our emotions are awakened when our parents are ill, or when they are taken from us. When we stare at the corner made vacant by their passing, then we know...but it is then too late.

There is one giver whose constancy is never broken and whose beneficence is therefore unnoticed by many, and he is Almighty God. Long before we come into the world, He has begun the process of forming us, of endowing us with the powers of body and mind that will unfold to yield a rich harvest through the years. The world which is our home, the very love of those near and dear to us, the capacity to dream, hope, love, work, build – these and countless other blessings are His gifts. Yet how many go through life using all these rich gifts without ever saying in word or thought: 'O Lord, I am grateful.'

Blessed are those who know the hand that feeds them. The food is then twice as sweet, because it also becomes a token of the Giver's love for man.

I SEEK MY FATHER

I seek God,
I seek Him with all my being,
My yearning is written
Into my inward parts.
Once I sought to still it
By building castles in the sand,
But one by one
I watched them crumble
With the passing days.

Then I looked deeper
Into my soul
And understood
Its endless craving.
I seek my Father
Who raised me from the dust
And gave me the breath of life.
As the plant turns
Toward the light
So I turn seeking
The Infinite.

In the longing of the heart
Is engraved,
You shall love the Lord your God
With all your heart,
With all your soul,
And with all your might.

The Way to Happiness

'LIVE a day at a time.' We have often heard this bit of wisdom, but it represents only a partial truth. Life has continuity and we cannot live from day to day, without planning ahead. The future is being formed in the womb of the present, and unless we weigh today's actions in terms of tomorrow's consequences we shall expose our lives to anarchy and improvisation. No significant result will ever reward our work, because any important enterprise requires time and planning for its proper conception and execution.

It is however true that for the enjoyment of life long stretches of time must be broken up into smaller units. From every day's labor, we must extract some measure of joy. We cannot defer our happiness to some spectacular fulfillment lying far away in time.

Life is a journey towards a constantly receding goal. We may succeed in grasping that for which we have reached, but we soon discover that something else beckons to us from the far horizon. We never reach a point where we may say: 'Now the race is run. I have found the heart's desire.' They who wait for these spectacular moments of

41

realization are doomed to unending frustration. And as the span of life is limited, we dare not put off to a far-away hour the rewards which we have a right to seek for our labors.

We must find life's fulfillment day by day. Every day has its own destination. Every day has its own struggles and attainments. Every day has its opportunities to taste from the sweet wine of life – by creative endeavor in work and play, by giving and receiving love, by serving God and man, by seeking after goodness and truth. Taste the wine when the cup is near. Who knows what tomorrow may bring?

Today's sunset will never again appear on the horizon. Today's opportunities for happiness will be gone when the day is done, and they will be gone beyond recall. Plan for tomorrow but do not forget to reap the harvest of this day.

Freedom

'It's a free world!' our seven-year-old son cried out in a final effort to rationalize his tantrum. He did not want to go to sleep, and he cried out against his enforced bed-time as an invasion of his rights. His illusion is not uncommon even among grown-ups. We often define freedom as the right to do as we please, but this is an erroneous conception.

Freedom is not the right to do as we please. No one can do just as he pleases, since we are all subject to pressure from sources beyond ourselves which cannot defy. If freedom consists of the right to that defiance under all circumstances, then none of us can be free. The laws of gravity, biology, geography; the laws of the road and of our home routines; the laws of the natural world and the laws of the man-made world – all these and countless other regulations limit our right to do as we please.

Freedom is the opportunity for self-realization. In each of us lie dormant all kinds of powers which were meant to be developed in the course of our maturing. And once developed, they were meant to be employed in the give and take of life. We are free if our powers can develop to the fullness of their promise and if we are unimpeded in their use.

A rock that rests on the seed planted in the ground will prevent its growth, thereby denying its freedom. But tying the tender plant to a garden stake – while limiting it from too much movement, rather than restricting – enlarges its freedom, because it is an aid to its growth. And a world in which little boys have to retire at a reasonable hour is indeed a world which holds the conditions of freedom, because it is in such a world that little boys can grow up to become wholesome and healthy adults.

Let us not fret because there are traffic laws by which we must travel on the highway of life. The laws of the road, if they make for safer driving, are a contribution to our freedom, not an infringement of it.

Space and Sympathies

Those who find themselves cloistered in too narrow a space often suffer from an affliction known as claustrophobia. It is the morbid dread of being shut in.

There is another kind of claustrophobia which occasionally afflicts people – a claustrophobia not of space but of sympathies. It is just as pernicious. There are some people who live only for themselves, all their thoughts, all their emotions are centered on their own egos. The house they live in may be a mansion of immense size, yet these people will suffer from the shut-in feeling.

A person expands or contracts the world to the dimensions of his own spirit. He whose sympathies reach out to other people finds his world enlarged to the measure of those sympathies. Through our broadened interests we can make ourselves part of all mankind, and rejoice in its past triumphs, struggle in its present dilemmas, anticipate its future hopes. People who do this are blessed, they live in the vast open spaces of the spirit.

Egocentric people are invariably troubled with a deep inner unrest. They feel that their lives are empty, as indeed they are. For they do not take enough of life into the circle of their interests. No one ego is sufficient to fill life with the meaning and purpose which is required to keep it going.

Egocentric people usually think they are being kind to themselves. They refuse to bestow themselves on others so that they may have more with which to serve themselves. But this is one of life's great illusions. For too much concentration on the self begets a shadow that obscures the rest of the world, and when we live with the image of that shadow constantly in our eyes, our spirit rises in revolt against its confinement.

Psychologists have called attention to a person's need to be loved. This is a valid need. But there is another truth which is occasionally overlooked. A person must not only receive love, he must also give it. A person who is concerned with himself alone will be truly miserable. Our interests must turn in both directions, out as well as in. Spoiled people are unhappy even though they are the recipients of love, because not enough of their love flows back into the world. A gift carries more blessing for the giver than for the recipient.

Our world is as big as our outlook. We crave to live in the larger world, not only of space but of sympathies.

Triumphant Living

To be healthy, wealthy, and wise is a wish frequently cherished by people. But did you ever consider that many who are blessed with these advantages often fail in making the most of their lives? In many instances, moreover, their failures are the direct consequences of their blessings.

Nothing is more dangerous to successful living than complacency, and people blessed with special advantages often become over-confident. They do not see the need for striving, because life's goals appear to them already won. But happiness does not lie in cherishing goals already won. It is rather in the struggle to realize them, in pitting one's strength against circumstances in order to forge something significant in ourselves, or in the world, that life takes on for us its vitality and interest.

There are deficiencies in all of us, and if the so-called 'blessed' will only look deeper into themselves and their world, they will find the imperfections against which to turn their energies. In this combat they will find the secret of triumphant living.

Roots

Gardeners will tell you that too much watering harms the lawn. If you watered too copiously, your plants would be content to get their nourishment from the earth's surface. They would not bother to grow roots deep enough to draw their supply from below. Further down, there is not only water but also precious mineral food of all kinds. The shallow living plants miss these, and grow into weaklings. The deeper the root, the sturdier the plant.

I have often reflected on this peculiarity of plants. Does it not correspond with human life? Affluence is often dangerous to its possessors. Only those who grapple arduously with life's problems develop these qualities or character – endurance, patience, the capacity to suffer privation. They are the sturdy plants in the world's garden. They have sucked up from its depths the nourishment which will help them face the rigors of life, fearlessly. Those who lack the incentive for striving, who find their needs supplied by a ready abundance, grow into weaklings.

People who have to struggle for their livelihood are spared this risk, since the normal course of their existence is sufficient to send their roots deeply into the soil of life and to give them the necessary toughening. Those who are affluent must also struggle. Theirs should be the greater privilege and the greater struggle – the struggle for ideals – for intellectual and moral growth, for the amelioration of the evils which beset their fellow men.

The roots must go deeper if the plant is to grow sturdier.

The Art of Love

The greatest of all arts is the art of love. We seek the well-being of those who are the objects of our affection. But how can we achieve this? Showering gifts on a child and allowing him to have his way at all times will not serve his well-being. It may even corrupt him and make him a mean and contemptible creature. On the other hand, thwarting him unduly may destroy his sense of security and cripple him emotionally for the rest of his life.

We need affection and the things it provides. But affection is not a green light permitting the ego to proceed without restraints. It expresses itself in giving, but also in denying, in caressing but also in rebuking. The instinctive self-seeking of the child will grow into the irrational compulsions of the adult unless as a child he learns that his will was meant to have reason as its master. By reason, I mean that which teaches a man to walk through life with humility.

He who has never been frustrated will become an insufferable brat whatever his age. Occasional frustrations are good for the soul. We cannot live in a civilized society and give vent to all the impulses that exist in our natures. Some of them must be vetoed; some of them must be frustrated; and some must be vetoed and frustrated at particular moments. Thus parents who frustrate their children's whims are not necessarily violating their love for them. In the right proportion, such frustrations may indeed be acts of genuine love.

About Books

Did you ever pause to marvel at the telephone, the phonograph, or the radio? I do not mean the intricate mechanism by which these devices operate, but the marvel of the service they render. These inventions enable you to escape from the limitations of time and space, so that you can hear and see people who are not physically present. Books are like that too. They are a recording of what some of the world's greatest masters have to say to us.

We cannot bring back to life a Moses, an Isaiah, a Lincoln, or a Spinoza. Yet these great people can still speak to us, reveal to us some of their innermost thoughts, by means of the printed page. A book enables you to roam freely in space and time and enter the company of the greatest people who walked this earth.

Some of us are afraid of great people, lest they be superior to us and we be unable to feel at home in their presence. For the same reason many of us shy away from great books, but when you get to know them, great people are human. It once took a little girl great courage to ask Albert Einstein to help with her arithmetic. He not only agreed, but they began a firm friendship.

Books are human too. Not all books can entrance you with the very first page. You have to give them time. You have to live with them, and read them. Allow them to develop their thoughts. Gradually you will feel their power and fall in love with them. The treasures of the printed page are like the treasures hidden in the earth, you have to do a little digging before you can bring them up to the surface.

Some of the greatest delights for the heart and mind

can come to you through books. If you have no books in your home, then bring them in. Every book is a window on the world, so why live in the dark when you can reach out for the light? And if you have books in your home, resting on the shelf, take them down and use them; don't let them collect dust. Books can be great friends. Take them with you on your journey through life.

The Measure of Responsibility

We need moderation in all things – even in our virtues. It is good to have a sense of responsibility, but if carried too far it will destroy our peace.

No man can carry the world on his shoulders. Our responsibility is limited by our capacity. Even our own private world often presents problems which we cannot readily handle. A person must do his best under all circumstances, and leave the rest to God. When we have done this we should be content. The outcome is not in our hands; and we cannot assume responsibility for it.

Some of us feel that it is incumbent upon us to safeguard our future, or the future of our children. We want to make plans that will reach far ahead into time and build round our vital interests a fortification which will make us impregnable to circumstances. And when we discover that we cannot do so, we become disturbed with a sense of insecurity.

Some of us have committed our energies in the service of some good cause, which has come to possess us. We would like to transform the world into the image of our ideal, but we find ourselves frustrated. The world will not listen, will not understand. Then, we may retreat, brokenhearted by defeat, or we break ourselves, trying to do the impossible.

But a man's responsibility does not extend to such extremes. We were meant to live with a measure of uncertainty. We cannot provide for tomorrow in tomorrow's entirety. When we have done the best we can, we must have faith that He Who gives us a new day will also give us the sustenance thereof. And we must have faith too that the cause which is so dear to us will not necessarily fail because at present the world appears indifferent to it. There will be others who will try again, another day.

You are not free to desist from the work; but it is not incumbent on you to finish it.

Tolerance

Tolerance is more than charity towards those who disagree with us. It is a duty we owe to ourselves.

What is the essence of tolerance? It is respect for the free expression of minds other than our own. Surely I do not possess perfect wisdom. My way of life reflects my own taste, my background of experience, what my limited knowledge has suggested to me as being sound and right. Because I am conscious of my limitations, I want other forms of life to flourish freely. It is their right, and I owe it to them. But I also owe it to myself, for how else will I ever correct my own deficiency except by permitting myself to be challenged by those who disagree with me?

A bigot is a source of misery to his fellow man, but he is also the forger of his own chains, jailing his soul from free contact with the world. He bites the hand that offers him food he has never tasted before, and which has new delights for the body or the mind.

A single flower could not contain within itself all the beauty and fragrance of the universe. This is why God has made many flowers in the garden of the universe. Woe unto the man who is so in love with the flower in his own window box that he would deny all others the right to be!

Man is the noblest flower in God's world. When you meet one with unfamiliar colour or character, don't trample on it. Cherish it as a new revelation of enriching beauty.

Tension of Adjustment

There is bound to be a measure of misunderstanding in every human relationship, for even the most ideally mated friends are distinct individuals, with unique mind and outlook on the world. Although reacting to the same experiences, we are bound to show different responses. From those differing responses arise occasional clashes of temperament, which produce bitterness and strife.

An ideal relationship is not one in which clashes never occur. Such a relationship is impossible; if it pretends to exist anywhere, it is because one individual entering the relationship is not truly himself. He may have suppressed his individuality for that of his more dominant partner, but one who lives in servility cannot fulfill the highest role of a mate, whether in friendship or in marriage, which is not only to commend but also to reprove; not only to acclaim but to challenge. The noblest mate is not one whose voice is an echo of our own; it is one whose voice blends with ours, while speaking with the uninhibited resonance of a free individual in action.

An ideal relationship is one where compatibility is achieved in the face of differences, where the two voices speaking in different tones are adjusted to blend in harmony, for the precise meaning of harmony is the readiness of differing elements to seek a higher unity by complementing each other instead of competing with each other. And if occasional clashes occur, true comrades on life's journey do not become alarmed, since such clashes are, for them, the tensions of adjustment rather than the explosions of open war.

Within a Boundary

A number of subtle forces contribute to our freedom. One of them is the fact of our limitations.

There is a common notion that to be free means to have the capacity of moving in any direction, without impediment or interference. But this is not altogether true. The young man who stands before the crossroads of his life, with many vocational opportunities beckoning him, is not really free. He is being crushed by too many pressures. He becomes free when he has resolved his dilemma and has accepted some limitation upon his life.

True freedom lies in expanding sufficiently to allow the fulfillment of one's possibilities. But growth can occur only in a particular direction. Among the conditions of freedom is the elimination of diversions, of distracting influences that would detour us away from the main course of our lives. Marriage commits a man to a particular woman. In that sense it is a limitation which contributes to freedom, for it releases a man from pursuing every attractive woman who crosses his path.

Life offers too many possibilities. The attempt to pursue them all would spell a tragic dissipation of our strength and frustrate our hope of great achievement. The elimination of alternatives, the reduction of our goals to manageable proportions, is a true prerequisite of freedom. Life can be free only when it is lived within a boundary.

Serve Life

The struggle against evil in ourselves and evil in our environment is often disheartening. We find these evils too firmly entrenched to prevail against. But have you ever tried to alter the tactics you use in this struggle? Have you ever tried, instead of attacking evil to strengthen goodness, which is its opposite?

Our most effective defense against disease lies not in fighting germs and toxins, but rather in the positive labor of improving health. A well-nourished and well-rested body can automatically resist the challenging adversary. The scales are always swaying between life and death. We can tip them in favor of life by increasing the elements which preserve life, so that the power of death is automatically curtailed.

It is more efficacious to serve life than to fight death. He who is orientated to the negative task of fighting against evil, sickness, and death has anchored himself in the swamp, and its foul odors will often depress him, but he who has set his heart to the positive service of extending life, faces the clean, open spaces which will exhilarate his spirit.

This is theory, but it is theory justified by experience. If you have wronged your fellow man, you will regain his goodwill by making up for that misdeed with overtures of kindness and friendship. The effort to undo what has already been done would be ineffective, and to persist would only cause growing anxiety. The foul air is withdrawn automatically when the windows are opened and the clear air blows in. There is no need to mobilize our energies in a positive campaign to expel the foul air.

As I consider myself, as I look at my world, I am often depressed. How deeply entrenched are the evils which depress me! What shall I do? Shall I organize a campaign to undo every thoughtless word or deed of mine? Shall I set myself to disprove every lie, to answer every word of malice spread in the world? Shall I reach out to seize and restrain the hand of every evildoer?

It is an impossible task. But I can serve my cause by positive deeds of goodness and truth. And He who ultimately judges and weighs the actions of men will know how to balance the scales. The realm of evil will recede by itself as the realm of goodness extends its sway.

We do not need to fight against darkness. When we kindle a light, the darkness is automatically vanquished.

Specialization

The world's work could not be done except through specialization. But specialization is also a great peril, for we each become so engrossed in the corner where we do our own work, that we are no longer aware of what goes on in the next corner.

The misunderstanding born of specialization is a universal

problem. The wife has her work and the husband his. Each work has its importance, and each its incidental griefs. But how many wives and husbands really understand each other?

The business man sneers at the professor, and the professor reciprocates. The scientist has a certain contempt for the minister, and the minister looks with suspicion on the scientist. The Army resents the Navy, and the Navy is condescending to the Army. Organizations serving different causes in the community see each other as competitors, rather than as partners and there is an unresolved tension among them.

Every person is in some respects a private world. Those outside cannot ever wholly lift the veil of individuality and one man can never completely know another's life, its joys, its works, its problems and heartaches. But he can try to understand, and when others talk about themselves, he can try to listen with sympathy.

We grow in understanding of the world as we grow in sympathy for its variety.

The Limits of Majorities

The truth can never be established by a majority vote. Every great idea in civilization began as a heresy, as a revolt against an established dogma in which the multitude implicitly believed. The pioneers who have advanced our knowledge and improved our lot were fundamentally, like father Abraham, idol breakers.

The exigencies of living together in the world force us to establish governments in accordance with the will of the majority. For man is a free agent and he must act voluntarily.

In his private life, he can choose his own course, but in the life of society he cannot choose alone, since he does not live alone. The majority vote is therefore the only safeguard of freedom. But it would be another matter if majorities were to determine our beliefs and opinions.

Majorities may, in the free exercise of their judgment, vote to make fools of themselves, but they have no right to silence the men who seek to remind them of their folly. The individual has only his own conscience to guide him in challenging the majority and proclaiming that it worships false gods. His proclamation may, of course, be misguided, but if we let ideas clash freely, a light will be generated at last by which we shall be able to distinguish truth from falsehood.

Those who would suppress ideas because they seem heretical to their own doctrine must either have a poor opinion of man, suspecting that he would fundamentally prefer error to truth, or they may be uncertain of their own doctrine, fearing its fate in the free clash of ideas.

Roughage

Our characters are never wholly black or wholly white. Our virtues and our vices are relative. There is some evil in the best of us, and some good in the worst of us.

An individual or a group may be judged to be dangerous to society. If such men organize a conspiracy to impose their will on the rest of their fellow citizens, they should be restrained by law. As long as their ideas remain in the realm of theory they should, however, be undisturbed. Their errors should be refuted while the possibility of truth in their theory should be sought from the mass of their discussions. We can make our truth richer, fuller, by learning from all men. Yes, we can learn even from views we judge to be erroneous.

The attempt to ban the writings of people simply because they entertain what we regard as pernicious doctrines is an instance of unwarranted tyranny. It will hurt not only its obvious victims, but also the society which rejects them. A total falsehood could never win support. Falsehood gains a following because it invariably contains an admixture of truth. This is the precious kernel we must save; the rest is husk to be discarded.

The bread we eat does not offer us food value alone. It also contains roughage. We should not be afraid of the roughage in the bread that sustains our minds any more than in the bread that sustains our bodies.

Pain for Gain

Living calls for the play of heroic qualities. At times these heroic qualities are summoned forth by an adversary, such as a human enemy against whom we struggle for prizes, real or imaginary, or an obstacle in nature we wish to subdue and bring under our control, such as an unexplored river or an unscaled mountain.

But we also need heroism in facing ourselves. The fiercest battle a man has to wage is against his own baser instincts, instincts which often imperil his nobler efforts. Fears, timidity, lethargy retard our efforts, and persist in whispering that there may be hazards in untrodden paths. And all these whispering agents represent a kind of fifth column inside our own hearts which serves the enemy's cause.

The invisible enemy who lurks, hidden, in us releases all the explosive emotions, like jealousy, anger, vengeance, which sap our strength, which cause deep divisions within ourselves as well as in the circle of our intimates. Like booby traps set by an enemy deep in our hearts, they go off with fierce and deadly eruptions, denying us the prize that might otherwise have been within our reach.

Heroism always involves a cool head, a precise understanding of the goal, an intelligent calculation of the effective steps towards attaining it, and the willingness to persevere, despite hardship. And heroism is an acceptance of pain for the sake of gain.

He who possesses these qualities can face any adversary, including himself. And he who can master himself is truly a hero.

Justice

The dream of all noble men and women through the ages has been of justice. Men have fought and men have died for it, yet the ideal must always remain impossible to realize.

What is justice? It is giving to each his due. But what is a man's due? No matter how you define it, it is impossible to draw a precise line to mark off the boundary of one life from another. And if we each persisted in seeking all that is due to us, the world would become embroiled in the endless friction of relentless claims and counter-claims.

Justice has sometimes been defined as a state of social organization in which each serves in accordance with his capacities, and is rewarded in accordance with his needs. But there is no ready determination of a man's capacities or of his needs. Only God can know the precise measure of man's abilities or of his requirements. Justice between men, then, can never be more than an approximation.

It is good to know that we have the right to expect from our world the opportunity to develop and use our distinctive talents and powers. The knowledge that this is our inherent right offers a valuable criterion for judging our world and man's destiny in it. But society could not endure if people knew no more than the self-centered virtue of claiming what belongs to them.

There is a virtue beyond justice that alone can help build a friendly world – and this is kindness, or love. A kindly person isn't worried about exact dues, but lives with his fellow man in a relationship of mutual helpfulness and mutual service. In God's world there is a mathematical balance, in which each is assigned a distinctive place. But the world that man must build can be sustained only by kindness, mercy, and love.

Don't Shrink From Challenges!

Have you ever travelled on the New Jersey Turnpike? It is a magnificent piece of road. Smooth, wide, without obstacles – it is built to fulfill the motorist's fondest dreams. Statistics, however, show that motoring on turnpikes like this is hazardous, and a disproportionately large percentage of accidents continue to occur on them. A recent report described these turnpikes as 'Speedways to Death.'

Why are these perfectly smooth highways so treacherous? Perhaps it is that they are too perfect! Driving for long stretches without hindrance causes drowsiness. Without challenge, without resistance, the mind becomes dull, the faculties dormant; the watchful eye goes off duty. The price of safety is constant vigilance, but there can be no vigilance except by contending with obstacles.

This is one of the important rules of all vital living. When life is too smooth, it becomes a boring business. This is why some people find life drab and uninteresting. They are too comfortable. A day comes and goes, but it flaunts no challenge in their faces. With dull monotony, they go through the day, without the stimulant of a battle fought and won.

Strive to aim high for yourself and for the world. Let your goal be great enough to test your best strength. Don't shrink from challenges, but welcome them warmly. In contending with challenges, we live life's most glorious hours.

It is good to meet an occasional obstacle on the highway of living.

When You Trip

'Naughty Chair!' the mother exclaimed, as she gave the offending chair a beating. After tripping over it, her little girl had cried inconsolably, but as she was beating it the child was soothed and her profuse tears gradually stopped flowing.

Why did the mother beat the chair? And why did this stop the little girl's tears? The chair had become a scapegoat. The little girl who had tripped through carelessness cried because her dignity was offended, and because she felt a little guilty for not having walked with greater care. By shifting the guilt from herself to the chair, she felt relieved because she no longer had to shoulder the blame for the mishap.

Isn't this a common weakness in which many of us indulge? We all tend to blame someone else for our troubles. We blame our husbands, our wives, our employers, our employees... We blame fate. We blame someone other than ourself for having caused our distress. Thus we save our pride, but we fail to profit by our mistakes.

That mother's stratagem saved her little girl some tears, but it failed in the more urgent task of teaching the child to accept herself and to live with the consequences of her actions.

Let us learn not to blame the chair – or anybody else – when we have tripped through carelessness. Only he who can admit his failures will learn to overcome them.

Shifting Into Reverse

Have you ever found yourself on a deadend road? You trusted yourself to it and hoped that it would lead you to your destination, but then you discovered, after some driving, that you were heading nowhere. There is of course a simple answer to such a predicament. You turn back and start again.

This is such a simple procedure but it involves a principle of great general importance. Life is not an irreversible movement. If you ever become convinced that the road on which you travel will not take you to your destination, then you can retrace your steps and start over again.

Living means experimentation. We cannot always be certain how our plans will turn out. We must do what seems plausible at first. But we may be mistaken; we may be embarking on a road leading nowhere. Many a man has had to change his business, his circle of friends, his style of living. Life is infinitely flexible, like the same clay out of which we make a variety of vessels, to suit the fancy of our visions.

However, it is not always easy to .turn back from a road which leads nowhere. The passage-way may be narrow, and turning round may involve difficult man-oeuvring. We regret, moreover, the time spent and the distance we have travelled in vain. Yet the law of the road demands that we turn back; and in such circumstances, turn we must. The pity of it is that some lack the courage, and remain in their deadend road, accepting their predicament, feeling sorry for themselves.

It is no reflection on our character that we have trusted ourselves, momentarily, to the wrong highway. Even the Lord destroyed a sinful humanity in a mighty flood, to start over again with the more promising Noah and his family. To miss the right road is human. It is less than human not to turn back.

There are men and women grieving by the wayside of life because they have become convinced that the road on which they travel leads to futility. Let them suppress their sighs and turn their hands to the wheel. We can always shift into reverse and retrace our steps.

The Maladjusted

The most fruitful source of human progress is man's capacity to feel maladjusted. If we were willing at all times to make our peace with circumstances, then we would never rise up in rebellion against the abuses that thwart us. We would probably still be one-celled animals living in the primeval swamp.

Progress begins when a man feels ill at ease in his world, when he refuses to accept his circumstances as something fixed to which he must adjust himself. There are times when man must adjust himself to the world, but the moments that have registered the greatest growth for the human race have been those moments when a man challenged the world and demanded that it should give way, that circumstances should adapt themselves to him rather than he to circumstances.

The maladjusted are often miserable. They are the people who are discontented with their lot. They are the dreamers of dreams, who reject reality in order to build it anew in the image of their dreams. They are often treated with scorn by their contemporaries who cling to their imperfect goods, without permitting dreams to disturb their peace of mind.

But those who are at peace when the world is full of imperfections will never lead humanity forward. Those who lead that forward march are the troubled, the discontented, the maladjusted.

The Overheated Car

The temperature gauge in your car is meant to guide you rather than to alarm you. When it shows that the car is overheated you are meant to slow down, to cool off, and so correct the condition.

And so it is with the operation of the gauges which control our lives. The most significant of these gauges implanted in ourselves is the conscience. It faithfully registers the condition resulting from our movements. There are times when it warns us that we are approaching a point of danger, persistently flashing its warnings and crying out that we are proceeding at great peril.

There are some people who, when they read the markings on the gauge, indulge in an orgy of self-pity, or else they begin the futile act of self-recrimination. They become obsessed with a sense of guilt, which in extreme cases may lead to a mental breakdown. For if the voices of accusation and indictment ring incessantly in our ears, their clamor becomes unbearable. He who talks incessantly, whether to himself or to the world, about his guilt, is a kind of hypochondriac. He insists on making his ailment the one predominant theme of his conversation.

The conscience was given us that it might induce us to redress our condition. If it flashes out a warning that we have gone wrong, then it summons us to return, to change, to take corrective measures.

If your car is overheated, don't sit by the road with folded arms, complaining about your fate. Correct the condition. A gauge is a device that makes for safer driving. Its purpose is not to emotionalize our occasional failures.

You Can't Forget

'Let's forget it.' Thus people often dismiss a misunderstanding. Yet it is essentially a false approach. For we cannot forget by simply wishing to do so. We forget only in words, but deep within, the rancor remains, and the shadow has not really been lifted. The invitation to forget is a pretense that something which occurred did not occur.

There is only one corrective to a misunderstanding and that is to cast more light on the issue. Every misunderstanding is based on a misinterpretation of motives. We see a deed or hear a word, which seems activated by unfriendliness. Then we cry out – not against the deed or the word, but against the unfriendliness. But another construction upon the facts is often possible which removes from them the overtones of malice.

Let those involved in a misunderstanding speak their minds fully and explain the facts that were judged offensive. Grievances vanish when misjudgments have been corrected.

Every reconciliation widens our capacity for friendship. On the other hand, the sterile effort to forget a grievance only succeeds in extending the rift. A veneer of friendly words cannot bury our lingering hurts.

Needs and Wants

There is a difference between needs and wants which we often overlook. A child cries: 'I want that candy.' He wants it, but he does not need it. A man says: 'I need a new car,' when he means he wants one; he may not need it. Most of the distress in life occurs because of this confusion. We want certain things, and then we persuade ourselves that we need them.

The things we want may or may not be necessary to our existence. They may be only superfluities of no consequence in our lives. But they may also be the very opposite of what we need – they may be the means of our injury. The card addict desperately wants to gamble, but he does not need to. What he needs is strength of character to avoid doing so.

The things which we really need we often do not want at all. The child needs food, but fights against eating. Is there anything we need more than a sense of integrity, or a clear conscience? Yet many people follow the tempting lure of some momentary gain, betraying what they need for the sake of immediate wants. Is there anything we need more than the peace of walking humbly with our God? Happy are they who have made this need the object of their wants as well, and who pursue it zealously. There are many who fight against God – as the sick man who fights against the medicine that will heal him.

Many of the things we want so desperately we could well do without. Some of them, we would indeed be better off without. On the other hand, many of the things we need urgently are well within our reach – if we would but want them. Fortunate are those who really need what they want, and who want what they need.

In Our Own Image

Every person tends to evoke from the world a reflection of himself. Your neighbor is gracious or abusive, very often, according to the way you have acted towards him. The dog is kindly or vicious, depending on whether you have shown him kindness or contempt. People and the world at large possess many different qualities of character, some higher and some lower. Our behaviour elicits the one or the other.

The world is not a constant, with a consistent reaction to what goes on in it, but a complex of adjustable phenomena which are responsive to every delicate mood in any of its creatures. Gentleness begets gentleness. Kindness will in the long run beget kindness. Similarly, viciousness will in the long run beget viciousness.

The world's response does not always occur instantly. The smile I show my neighbour may not immediately bring the response I seek, since an accumulated bitterness may have formed in him a frown that he cannot readily discard. But no smile of mine will be wholly lost. The ice thaws gradually, but every ray of sunshine contributes to the thawing. And every expression of regard I show my neighbour will have the same effect. It will cause a thawing of his rigid indifference, provided my gestures are sincere and persistent enough. We build, by our actions, in the people around us cowardice or heroism, nobility or meanness.

The town you live in consists of friendly or unfriendly people, depending in part on what you have made of them.

Self Control

The key to human survival is restraint. Have you ever reflected on the tremendous energies which lie imprisoned within the atom and on what would happen if these energies ever escaped their prison? Our planet would die in one gigantic catastrophe of unimaginable terror. Our planet survives and we survive in it because these energies stay contained in the atom.

There are powers of immense terror lurking in the human heart, and they too require keeping under control if man is to survive. During fits of jealousy, hatred, anger, people have revealed the convulsions of vast and terrible pressures. If the explosions of the atom have devastated Hiroshima, have not the explosions of anger, of hate, of jealousy proven as deadly? Many a life has been ruined, many a home broken, because of the violence released by fierce emotions raging deep inside us.

The survival of man depends on regulating those emotions. We say to a person on the verge of excessive excitement : 'Contain yourself,' and it is an injunction of great importance. A hero is he who masters his emotions, because he thereby saves himself no less than the one who exasperates him.

Contain your anger; contain your jealousy; contain the fires of suspicion and envy that you feel igniting within you. They may spread into a mighty conflagration beyond your ability to control. By containing them you will save your life, your home, your business, yes, your world.

IT IS ENOUGH

There is joy enough to stand awed
At the vast baffling world,
To be enthralled by a sunset
To feel the terror of storm
To marvel at decline and rebirth
In the rhythm of nature
And in the ebb and flow of my own life.

It is enough to hear the sound of laughter,
The whispered exchange of lovers,
The cadence of words spoken in friendship.
It is enough to hear a cry of pain
And feel charged to heal it
With soft words and loving deeds
That bind man to man,
Brother to brother.

God's Plan

SIMON mourned excessively for his departed friend. He was inconsolable in his grief. One night in a vision he heard a voice say to him reprovingly: 'Why do you grieve so much? Is not death an inevitable incident in the cycle of life? Would you change the plan of the universe and make man immortal?'

Simon gathered courage and he replied: 'Why not, O Lord? Thou canst do all things. Why should there be an end to lives as wonderful as that of my friend and others like him?'

And the voice replied: 'So you deny the service of death to the economy of life. Very well, then. We shall set your feet upon an immortal world, and see how you like it.'

Simon looked at this new countryside and thought of the promises of his dream, that all its magnificence would endure for ever, nothing of it would perish. And indeed so it turned out.

Not a flower died on its stalk. Not a blossom fell from the lilac bushes. Summer gave way and autumn came, but not a leaf withered, not a tree lost its foliage. The world in all its beauty had been given a kind of fixed permanence, and it shone in the self-same luster. At last life seemed to be freed from the ravages of time and circumstance.

But gradually it palled on Simon. Nothing died in his world, but nothing was born in it either. He was spared the ravages of age, but he missed seeing the wondrous dance of youth. His eyes tired at the beauty of flowers forever the same in hue. He longed to witness the glory of a new flower's unfolding. He was ready to renounce the gift of immortality when he suddenly awoke from his dream.

He brooded for a while over his strange experience and then he said: 'O Lord, I thank Thee that Thou hast made us mortal. Someone died that I might be born and I am willing to die that there may be growth and the emergence of new life in Thy world. Thou art a righteous Judge.'

The Quest for the Beautiful

I have never met the architect who designed the house I live in, but by contemplating his work I can discern a good deal about the bent of his mind. And so it is that, never having seen God, I may yet know His ways. I can discern it by contemplating this vast world which is His creation.

I know that God loves beauty, for He allows it to flourish everywhere, even in unexpected places. In the woods He has scattered all kinds of wild flowers. In a ruin wrought by men, who have cut down beautiful trees and left the brush in disorder, the Creator has caused the ungainly sight to be covered over with a verdant growth: raspberry bushes have come up and new trees are growing. It is He who made the sunrise and the sunset, the towering mountains, and the sharp drop of the lowlands. He made the birds with the infinite variety of their plumage, and He wrought a child's smile.

I know too that God loves beauty, because He placed the love of beauty in the human heart. He inspired the vision of artists, from whose soul the beauty of the world evokes the resonance of a new beauty, of their own creating. And even those who are not so deeply inspired know instinctively how to choose the beautiful and to shun the ugly.

The fruit on the topmost branch of the tree was already contained in the seed from which the tree unfolded. And whatever surges in the world and in man, must have come, from the very root of its being, from its Creator.

And if God loves beauty, then one way of adoring Him is by our own quest for the beautiful. To overcome disorder and ugliness, to extend the sway of the beautiful, to create new beauty and to cherish it, must be acceptable to the Lord. Emulation is the highest tribute to God, as well as to man.

I Have Heard the Song

I have not seen the robin but I know he is there because I heard him singing through my window from the tree-top outside.

I have not seen God. But I have looked at my child's eyes, and have been overwhelmed by the miracle of unfolding life.

I have watched the trees bedeck themselves with new garbs of green in the spring, and have been stirred by the miracle of continual rebirth.

I have looked at the stars, and have been overcome by the miracle of the grandeur and majesty of the universe.

I know that God exists, because I have heard the song of His presence from all the tree-tops of creation.

The Fruit Must Ripen

One can never judge an edifice before the workmen's scaffolding has been removed, and the final touches of work have been executed, for an incomplete operation can never reveal the excellence of the underlying plan.

The criticisms levelled against the world invariably overlook this principle. The world was not perfected at the time of creation.

A finished world would have left no room for progress, and it would have destroyed man's most thrilling experience, the striving for perfection. Because the world included vast realms of disorder, man has been given ample scope to work with hand and heart, to build in the image of his dreams.

The world, if it is to remain a fit place for human life, will have to retain some elements of imperfection to challenge man's initiative, otherwise stagnation will set in, and life wither away through insufferable boredom and inanity.

Much of the evil that now ravages mankind will, undoubtedly, be overcome. It may be that men will continue to contend with each other, as a result of their different outlook on the world, but they can contend, as friends do, in a spirit of good will, without resorting to violence.

The evils which now dishearten us are to a great extent the result of the world's immaturity. Humanity is still young, and if we are stumbling and often falling, it does not mean that we will not learn to stand erect, and to walk as men should, without tripping.

We shall have to wait a little longer for the uncompleted design of the world to reveal its true quality. A fruit is usually bitter before ripening.

We Are Healed While We Sleep

One of the greatest landmarks in medicine was the development of anaesthesia. During the time of induced slumber, the most delicate acts of surgery may be performed. Our flesh is cut and we feel no pain; we are healed while we sleep. Thus man imitates his Maker.

For is not this ministry of healing performed every day of our lives? At the end of each day our bones ache, our muscles are tired, our bodies and minds have suffered all kinds of bruises in their encounter with the world. Then we retire for the night, and during the hours of sleep the divine Healer attends to us and brings us relief. We arise each morning restored and refreshed, strengthened for the tasks of a new day. We have been healed while we were asleep.

The Existence of God

Sensitive people need to believe in the existence of God, in order to understand the world. The purpose and order and beauty of creation leaves them with the over-powering conviction that some guiding Intelligence, of infinite power, wisdom and goodness, is behind it all. The void that would be created by the surrender of this conviction would make our world totally irrational.

But the belief in the existence of God fills another need for sensitive people. It helps them find meaning in their own existence. No one can meet the challenging demands of living without the sustaining faith that one's work serves some abiding purpose. But what purpose of mine can have abiding significance unless there is significance in the entire drama of life in which it plays a part? Unless this be so, every individual episode within it is doomed to frustration, regardless of outcome.

The individual passengers aboard a ship cannot be sailing towards a destination unless the ship itself is being steered by some captain's hand. Otherwise, the ship will only drift. It will battle against the waves, but it will find no haven.

Old Blankets

A child will clutch an old blanket or an old and battered toy, and will not let it go. He takes it with him to bed, as though it were his most priceless possession. Parents are occasionally baffled, but the child is only affirming a principle that dominates all life. He is attached to the familiar.

Amidst the shifting things which make up the world of common experience, it is comforting to hold on to something which does not change. It gives us a feeling of stability and permanence. The blanket is precious precisely because it is old and worn, because around it cluster many sweet memories of being tucked into it by the tender and loving hands of mother, night after night. The blanket is an anchor that holds the tiny ship to the shore, while yet permitting it to venture a little way in slow motions of discovery and exploration.

We all clutch old blankets of one kind or another. We feel a special attachment to objects, and places, and people, because they carry happy memories for us. We hold on to ideas and persist in habits because they carry the compulsion of the familiar.

This compulsion of the familiar may be injurious. It makes it difficult for us to grow up, to change, to respond to the call of new ideas. Yet we could not meet life's demands without it. For this is the source of our loyalty to all that we have and all that we are. It gives us a feeling of security and permanence, amidst the anarchy of change which we see all about us.

The attachment to the familiar is a device that God has put into our natures, to make sure that we shall live in the three dimensions of time. We are moving from the present into the future, and we were meant to take our past with us.

God's Ever Seeing Eye

How can God know my thoughts before I conceive them?

He knows them because a Creator knows His creation with an intimacy which is denied to onlookers.

An architect knows the characteristics of an edifice he has designed, and he can predict its strength as well as its weakness long before the edifice is put to use. An outsider's knowledge is synthetic. It is based on observation, and it is always after the event. He who has internal knowledge can know events before they transpire, because he understands the forces which underlie such actions.

A thought, a deed, is only the expression of a soul. Whoso knows the soul, knows the thought and the deed; and he knows them even before their fullest unfolding.

Those who understand the psychology of a child can chart his reactions even before he is born, estimating how he will behave at the moment of birth, at five or at fifteen. A gardener knows from the seed how each flower will blossom, and when. And even when the butterfly is only a cocoon or a crawling larva, we know that some day it will grow wings and soar towards the heights.

God has given each of us the freedom to mold out of the raw material of our lives the kind of characters we want to be. But God knows the nature of those raw materials and He stands with us as a co-worker in the designing of our lives, helping us to shape the form we want it to hold. He knows our soul and therefore He knows the thoughts and the deeds which spring from it.

Let no man ever say: I can think whatever I please, I can do whatever I please, no one sees me. For there may be no man near but God looks upon us always.

Shut Doors

Rivers are created by a confluence of water from springs or from deposits left by the rains or snow on the mountain tops. And a river is shaped by the natural boundaries on each side. These boundaries keep the water from spreading out and dissipating into the surrounding land, and as the inflow continues, a course is marked on which the river moves endlessly forward.

The movement of life is not unlike the movement of a river. The spring from which we receive the precious essence of our existence, the resources of our being, is the fathomless depth from which all life comes. It is the chain of our ancestry remolded by the unseen hand of the Creator. Out of these raw materials we mold the personalities that we finally become.

But we move forward not only because of our endowments. We move forward also because of our limitations, which set a boundary keeping us from dissipating ourselves over too wide an area. Unlimited endowments would open to us too many possibilities, and we would be tempted to dabble in too many realms. It is easier to concentrate on one goal when other horizons do not beckon, tempt and lure.

Let us not fret then because we are limited. We are each limited in some respects and endowed in others. Our limitations really simplify our task, by setting the boundaries within which we were meant to confine the movement of our lives. It is easier to choose when our choice has been narrowed to manageable proportions. It is good that some of life's doors are shut in our face. It facilitates our finding the open door through which we were meant to walk.

They Were Meant to be Collaborators

It is well that a car is equipped with brakes. Otherwise, it would speed away out of our control.

The Lord ordered the world similarly. Some people he made dreamers, investing them with a vivid imagination to see all kinds of visions. They are impatient with their surroundings and are ever eager to speed off to some promised land beyond the horizon.

If these people were unchecked, they would destroy

life's stability. They would forever be stampeding us to all kinds of fanciful realms, where our lives could not be sustained. The Lord therefore provided a brake, in people who are stern realists, who will puncture every dream with the needle of keen analysis, who will challenge every vision in the name of fact and circumstance.

Between the dreamers and the stern realists there is an unending feud. For the realists are always putting a brake on the dream and checking the speed with which we might move towards it. The feud may be bitter. For the realists judge the dreamers to be the enemies of society. Indeed, history knows instances where the dreamers seized control and turned fanatic, destroying those who were not ready to join in their adventure.

A healthy society is one in which the dreamer recognizes the right to be challenged in the name of realism, and in which the realist recognizes the right to be questioned, in the name of progress.

The dreamer and the realist were meant to be collaborators. Through the balance of their conflicting pressures we forge an ordered progress in which we shall reach out towards new goals, without sacrificing settled achievements.

The Course of the Stars

There are some forty thousand million stars in the Milky Way. All of them are in endless and precise motion, each keeping his unfailing place in the highway of the heavens.

And millions of stars in other groupings reveal no less grandeur, no less order and precision in their awe-inspiring movements. Can it be that these movements occur without a directing hand of an infinitely wise and powerful Intelligence?

The traffic on the highway near my home moves smoothly because a policeman directs it. If the order of the moving cars on the highway is a product of a guiding hand, can it be that the motions of the stars proceed at random, without a directing hand to set them and keep them in their courses in space?

Watching the stars in their course in the sky, I am overcome with awe at the glorious majesty of God Who continues to sustain all realms of life in the universe, in the harmonious fulfillment of their appointed purpose.

Tipping the Scales

He had finished reading the newspaper, and had fallen asleep, still depressed by the usual reports of horror in the world.

Then he dreamed that he saw before him two colossal scales. In one there was an enormous bundle marked with the sign, 'The sins of humanity.' In the other there was another bundle of equal size marked with the sign, 'The virtues of humanity.' The scales were perfectly balanced.

At once he was alarmed by the precarious condition of humanity, and he felt that it was up to him to save the world from impending doom. He decided to remove some of the weight from the bundle of sin. He pitted his full strength against the massive bundle of sin, but could not move it. He tried to cut off a portion with an axe, but it stood like granite, impervious to his efforts.

Then he felt forlorn, for himself and for his world. But in the moment of his greatest dejection he heard a voice

speaking to him: 'Stand on your feet and despair not. Once
a sin has been committed, it is difficult to undo it, but you
can still save yourself and your world. Go out and do a
good deed, and it will be placed in the bundle of the
world's virtues.'

At that point in his dreams a storm broke outside and
he heard a woman's voice crying in the night. He opened
the door and gave her shelter till the storm had passed.
And with this gesture of kindness he saw the scales tipping
in favour of virtue.

He was watching the swaying scales with satisfaction,
when he was aroused from his reveries. The newspaper was
still before him. He looked at it, mused for a while, then
thrust it disdainfully into the waste basket, and with determination proceeded to the next task which summoned him.

No Day Is Nasty

'What a nasty day,' the man muttered under his breath.
He was annoyed because it was raining and the sun was
hidden away beneath the clouds. But was this not a foolish
complaint?

The world needs the rain as much as the sunshine. Every
tree and flower and blade of grass had prayed for this
rain. The earth itself had gone dry and had yearned for
water to be refreshed. And in the carefully balanced
economy of God's world, there may have been multitudes
of other needs which that rain satisfied.

We sometimes assume that the whole world ought to
revolve 'round our private whims and wishes. But the
Lord knows better than to listen to our prayers when they
are foolish. For are not prayers foolish when they ask what

we, with our limited foresight, wish to take precedence over God's plan which is best for the whole universe? If there is a conflict between what is good for the universe and what we think is good for us, then let God's will be done, rather than ours. It is we who must adjust ourselves to God's plan. We cannot expect that plan to be adjusted to our private desires.

There are no nasty days. We can make them so if we do not use them to their full advantage. But every day as it proceeds from its womb of time is a fresh creation of God. And whatever the Lord has made is good.

The Bridge to Our Dreams

The New Year was fast approaching, and Simon felt possessed by a mood of introspection. He looked at the mirror – not the one of silvered glass, but the one that reflected his mind – and what he saw filled him with a sense of panic. All his foolish and rash acts of the past year passed before him, and he felt humiliated. All lost opportunities too passed before him, each suggesting something wonderful that might have been, and he felt remorseful.

With these melancholy thoughts, he fell asleep while still in his chair, and was startled by a strange vision. It came to him clear as the noon-day, but it was only a dream.

He saw himself, marching towards the far horizon which was shot through with the pale gold of the rising sun, until he came to a river, turbulent and swiftly moving, with jutting rocks and frightening falls, which he tried in vain to pass. Then he became aware that he was carrying a bundle. He tried to drop it, but could not. It was part of him, like a member of his body. On examining it closely he could make out a sign which read: 'Every man's folly becomes part of the burden he carries on his journey through life.'

If only he could have dropped the bundle he was sure he would be able to navigate the river. But now he felt himself barred. The pale gold of the beckoning horizon drew him like a magnet, but he could not go on. Dejected, he broke down and cried.

Suddenly he heard a still small voice speaking to him: 'Cry, Simon, cry! Many a man has seen more through a tear than through a telescope. Stop trying to drop your bundle. What is done cannot be undone. But you can build a bridge across the river. Every good deed you do becomes a plank, from shore to shore. Stop worrying about your follies, concentrate on the good that you can yet do and you will build a bridge to the land of your dreams.'

At that point he woke up. He mused for a while. Then a broad smile settled on his face, as he got up from the chair, and with lighter step, he proceeded about his business.

Growth is an Unseen Mystery

The other day I watched my eight-year-old son swing a bat at the approaching ball. He looked quite grown up among his team of playmates. When did this miracle of growth occur? As I look back I can see him at various stages, but I can see no more than the results of a change. The act of changing can never be seen with the naked eye. Today we are one thing; tomorrow, another. The transformation is an unseen mystery.

Growth is usually slow. No one sees the flower's blossoming. No one sees the formation of a new ring in the trunk of a tree, marking the passage of another year. We can only see what is. But in the womb of the present the unseen mystery of growth is acting itself out, slowly and imperceptibly. And when the transformation is complete, the future emerges.

The fact that growth is an unseen mystery is one of our great sources of hope in the world. We look at ourselves and at our world, and we are often discouraged by what we see, and by what appears to be our prospect. We can discern no turn in life's direction towards the dreams we have cherished and worked for.

But we could never discern life's changing direction with the naked eye. These turns are often the unseen mystery of growth. And while we deplore some deficiency lurking in the present, a brighter dawn may, unnoticed, be upon the horizon. One day we wake up and, startled by the change, wonder when and how it all happened. Then we will become conscious of one of the many wonders in the baffling mystery of life.

The Blind Child

The Creator had resolved to usher into the world a new life. He endowed the tiny infant boy with many precious attributes of heart and mind. But that infant was to lack one very important attribute – that of sight. Even the Creator is to some extent limited by the laws which He established in this universe. Under the circumstances of its conception and pre-natal development, this child had but two grim alternatives – to die before coming into the world or to live without physical sight.

The child was born blind, and when his parents discovered it, they grieved incessantly. One day when the mother was especially sad over her misfortune, her blind baby looked up to her. And though the baby's eyes could not see, they somehow compelled the mother to listen attentively.

'Why do you cry? Will that make me see? For me the choice was to be denied life altogether, or to be denied one attribute of life – my vision. If you really love me, then join with me in thanking God for my narrow escape. I will need all your love to help me make the most of the attributes I do possess. I shall not be able to see with the eye of the body, but I will have to learn to see with my heart and my mind. God Who has given me life will do His share, and I know that in a thousand ways, He will give me strength to compensate for my weakness. Will you do your share?'

The mother bent over her sightless son and kissed him tenderly. And in a voice choking with emotion but now resolute with determination, she said: 'No, I will not fail you. I shall try to do my share.'

God Is One

Words are an ingenious tool of the human spirit, but they are often misused. We tend to color their meaning with all kinds of personal references, not intended by those pronouncing them, and then these words become a source of confusion rather than of clarity.

Who is not familiar with the statement: God is One? But what does the Oneness of God really mean? Most of us apply numbers to the tangible objects of the world. We therefore apply the number one to God in the same sense. We say that there is only one God in the world in the same way we might, theoretically, say that there is only one apple in the world, regarding the world as a kind of tremendous bag which contains many things. It contains more than one of such things as: apples, people, animals, rocks and plants, but the entity we call God is unique; there is only one.

This is an absurd error. The world is not greater than God so that it cannot contain Him. Space is one of His creations, and He existed before space was born.

The world cannot contain God but God can and does contain the world. He contains it in the literal sense of the term, derived from the Latin and meaning *to hold together*. Only physical objects occupy space. The characteristics of physical objects do not apply to God.

When we say that God is one we mean that one intelligence integrates the total drama of existence. The life and death of a star or of a blade of grass, the countless creatures in this world, in their diversity, reflect the work of one will, one law, one design.

The essence, the nature of this Being is beyond our mortal minds, but His existence is made manifest everywhere throughout that design which is creation.

To unravel as far as possible that design underlying the universe, and to attempt to live in accordance with it, is for man the noblest goal to which he can commit his energies.

Divine Discontent

The commodity which man seeks most avidly at every counter of life is peace of mind. Wistfully, we dream of being at ease, without deep anxieties or distresses to disturb our spirits. There is reason, however, to argue that peace of mind was not meant to be a vital ingredient of our happiness.

A mind that is totally undisturbed would be a mind that can no longer feel the sense of challenge. Static water can readily become stagnant, and a life of perfect ease would be a life without the incentive to strive in new directions. The inspiration to every movement in a new direction is always some discontent with the present position. It is only when we are disturbed that we become alive to the need for action, and only then, in response to that need, does there flow into us the vital new energy to do great things.

People of our time have lost the capacity to find pleasure in their discontent. In part, it is because they have lost faith in God. For when we believe in God and in His purposeful government of the world, we can see a purpose even in our disturbance. Without God the world is soulless and indifferent to human hopes. In such a world, everything seems futile except momentary pleasure.

A momentary pleasure cannot yield happiness. The moment we became disturbed with the sense of our deficiency may be the moment when God has conferred upon us His greatest gift – an invitation to reach out for new possibilities. It is in accepting these invitations that we achieve the enduring satisfactions of life.

New Grapes

Life moves in a cycle, and destruction is an essential incident in it. No new grapes would grow on the vine, unless the old grapes were removed. They may be removed by man, when they are ripe, to make wine of them, otherwise, they will rot and fall by themselves.

The forces that produce this rottenness, the fermentation and decay which disintegrates all substances, are always active in the world. When an organism is in its prime it has sufficient resilience to resist these forces. The power of growth and stability which is a continuation of the miracle of creation vanquishes for a time the forces of disintegration and allows life to go on. But when an organism's resilience has diminished as a result of injury or because it has fulfilled its allotted time on earth, the power of disintegration is permitted to do its work unchecked.

The ferment of disintegration is a social force also. The Creator did not want social institutions to remain rigidly fixed and immobile. He wanted men to grow new grapes on the vine. Therefore did the Lord endow some people with a tendency to tear down existing institutions. They are critics, fault-finders, rebels. They are the element of decomposition which ferments society. They prevail only when society has lost its resilience, when an internal sickness, engendered by persistent abuses, has destroyed its health. A healthy society will know how to defend itself against the darts of their criticism. But some social institutions deserve to be fermented, to be undermined, and the force that challenges them and lays bare their weaknesses is performing a useful purpose.

When we accept life and rejoice in it, it is well to

remember that life is a cycle of change and that included in the cycle also is disintegration and death.

Wisdom and Moderation

God or the world? Man has often been challenged to choose between these two, but the challenge is based on a false philosophy. It is based on the notion that the world is evil, and that loving the things of the world must also be evil. But how can the world be evil if God created it? How can loving any of God's creations be evil in His sight?

No, man dare not shun the world. It is the home into which he was placed. To turn our backs on it would be to reject what the Lord has given. Man has a duty to plant and harvest, to build and create, to exchange goods and services, to explore nature and master her ways, to fashion for himself objects of beauty as well as utility, to find a mate and marry, to beget children and rear them, to strive with others in developing the furniture of civilization.

Absorption in the pursuits of the world may become evil if carried to excess. The hunger for material things may capture a man's total interest and thereby make a slave of him; the hunger for sexual gratification, if abused, may push him down the road of dissipation and destroy his strength. These perils exist. They only emphasize the need to direct our pursuits with wisdom and moderation. They do not point to the need to shun the world as a snare.

There are evils in the world because men have not yet mastered the art of living. When they master it, they will vanquish those evils. To do this is part of the mission confronting man on earth.

The Language of Poetry

Have you ever examined your speech with any kind of care? All of us constantly say things we cannot mean, at least not literally.

We speak of a fork in the road, of the foot of a mountain, of the mouth of a river. The poet has even suggested to us that a tree has leafy arms which are lifted towards God in prayer. Such speech is of course only figurative. Scenes of nature are made more vivid by being compared to something which is intimately close to us in human experience.

The most daring instance of figurative speech is illustrated in our reference to God. We speak of the hand of God, the mouth of God, the eye of God. God is not a physical body, and He is therefore without physical organs. We ascribe such organs only in a figurative sense.

The hand of God is a figurative term for God's power, since, in human experience it is the most common wielder of power.

The mouth is the human means of communication. When we wish to convey that some vision of beauty, some concept of truth, was inspired by God, we sometimes say, as the prophets do, that the mouth of the Lord had spoken it. But God conveys His inspiration without the play of physical instruments.

The eye is the most obvious organ for the exercise of human care. When we ask a neighbor to keep an eye on our child we mean that we want her to be mindful of his welfare. In a figurative sense, we associate the eye with God also. We say, for instance, that the eyes of the Lord are on those who revere Him, when we mean that God protects them.

We must not confuse the literal with the figurative meaning in our speech, if we wish to avoid the most absurd errors. Poetry abounds·in figurative speech. The language of a religion is a language of poetry.

And all these figures of speech we apply to God spell the conviction that He has the power to perform His will, that He illumines certain chosen spirits with the truth of His being, and that He is concerned with the destinies of His creatures.

Is Sex Sinful?

Certain moralists have spoken disparagingly of the sexual impulse. They have summoned people to suppress this impulse as something sinful. But they are tragically mistaken.

God is the author of life, and whatever He has put into our natures must have a useful purpose. The useful purpose may, of course, be overlooked, for the freedom which is man's condition in the world allows him to employ his impulses in one way or another. The legitimate use of any impulse is good. To abuse it is sinful.

There are no good or bad impulses. The impulse to love is not necessarily good, and the impulse to hate is not necessarily sinful. If we love what is unworthy of love, then our love is evil. On the other hand, if we hate what is really reprehensible then our hatred is commendable. The noblest spirits of the human race have been people who have known great hatred – they have hated shams, falsehood, and every form of wrong-doing.

Every impulse is a clue to a path which the Creator wanted us to travel. The presence of the sex impulse is an indication that God wanted men and women to be mated, and to beget children, the choice fruit of their mating. Marriage and family life are a fulfillment of God's plan for mankind. The sexual impulse is the device the Lord planted in His creatures so that His plan shall not be frustrated.

The fact that some people over-eat is not an argument against eating. Some people have abused the sex impulse and made of it a means to perverted gratifications, but this does not argue the sinfulness of sex.

Why Am I Ashamed?

We may deny God in words, but we cannot help affirming Him in our deeds. Why do I feel embarrassment each time I recall an equivocal deed of mine? No one knows, and I am immune from its consequences. But the self-knowledge that I have transgressed some vital rule of decency continues to make me ashamed. I may push that memory back into the subconscious. But I cannot persuade the One who speaks to me, through the voice within, to approve of it.

The continuous operation of the conscience is an indication that the ultimate reality of the universe upholds decency. For is not my life only a spark of the life of the universe, and is not the pulse which beats in me a clue to the things which propel all life? If the world were moved only by blind force, conscience would be out of place in it.

The presence of a conscience that discriminates between right and wrong is a manifestation of a universal Power concerned with righteousness, operating at the heart of, the universe.

The Fascination of the Unfamiliar

Fishing is good when raindrops fall. Living in the very midst of water, the fish will nevertheless rise to the surface because of the exciting possibility of catching a drop from the outside. It is not that the fish is short of water in his river or ocean, but he apparently fears he will miss something different which has come his way. There is allure in the unfamiliar.

The fascination of the unfamiliar is often a source of trouble in life. It makes us on occasions spurn the riches at hand for the dubious goods that are being sold at some alien counter. It is the source of much of the discontent which robs us of our peace. Yet is this not also one of the glorious qualities of life?

The fascination of the unfamiliar has inspired us to explore new realms of experience. It makes us adventurous, inquisitive, daring. It prevents smugness, complacency, and inertia.

In the limited life of a fish, a drop of rain is a symbol of a world beyond the frontier. It is a symbol of the eternal fascination of the unfamiliar which is felt deeply by all God's creatures. Not every land beyond the frontier is better than our own surrounding countryside. But it is good that we feel the impulse to explore.

Not Blind Chance

Winter in its forbidding austerity is coming upon our world. Soon the paralysis of cold will strike. Soon nature will cover its growing glory with a mask of snow. I can see the birds in their migrations southward, seeking the comforts of a warmer home.

Who taught the birds to follow the journey south? Who mapped out their itinerary? Who gave them the spirit of adventure to follow the promise of a better life, and who gives them the wisdom to find their way back again when the winter is ended and a warm sun shines on our world once more?

When I contemplate the wonder of the birds I know that Thou, O Lord, dost guide it all. Not blind chance but a plan of infinite wisdom governs the life of the universe.

IN A CIRCLE

A father allows his child
To fall
That he might raise himself
And learn to walk on his own feet.
Man was sent
To wander in the world
And learn
In the school of suffering
To choose
His way.

Man lives in a circle.
He falls away from God,
Then struggles
To return to Him.
He leaves the Eden of his beginning
To build another Eden
By tracing
God's blueprint
On the design of his life.

We Can Choose Ourselves

WE cannot choose our parents, but we can choose our-selves. Some basic elements in our personalities are, to be sure, assigned to us. We receive from the accumulated reservoir of our heredity and from the undetermined trea-sury of God's free gifts many of the vital ingredients that enter into the making of our lives. But the fact remains that a reservation has been left open for us to exercise ample freedom in fashioning ourselves into the kind of people we would like to become.

Poverty or riches, sickness or sound health, the presence or absence of talent, education or the lack of it, the pressures of the society into which we are born—these in themselves do not make a man. Heroes as well as villains have emerged out of apparently identical circumstances. For circum-stances are only raw materials, which condition, but never determine, the object that is finally wrought. The final element of determination is the vision towards which we build. It is the model which inspires our labors.

Let a man know what he wants to become. Let him hold on to this ideal, and make it the blueprint that guides his work. This vision, and the will to serve it, will mold the ultimate quality of our lives. It enables every man to grow towards the image of his own dream.

A Sense of Security

The sense of security is an indispensable need for emotional health. But what is it that can make a person feel secure in the world? Our parents have often been held responsible for developing it in us. The love of a father and a mother creates in the child the feeling of being wanted, filling the child's world with warmth. Thus is engendered the sense of security which we all need for a happy response to the rigorous demands of living.

There is no question that parental love will add to the child's feeling of security in the world, particularly for the very young child. Yet parental love is an insufficient anchor for emotional security. For our parents are mortal, and we are bound to lose them. And even while we have them, they do not always afford us enough anchorage in life, for as we grow in understanding, we realize that our parents are but finite creatures and limited in the resources of wisdom and strength with which to support our own lives. We need another love to reinforce parental love if we are to have durable sources of security for living.

The love which time cannot undermine, and which is available to under-gird us in our need for feeling at home in the world, is the love of God. One who recognizes God's love is emotionally fortified for the strenuous business of living. For his sense of security is based on unshakable foundations.

The Invisible Environment

A man's life is conditioned by his environment, both visible and invisible. The visible environment consists of the external things and external events in which our lives are set. The invisible environment consists of the ideas which inhabit our minds.

At any given time, our minds are saturated with ideas of one kind or another. We think of honor or dishonor, of courage or failure. We think of our material needs or of our spiritual deficiencies. We dream of service to our fellow man or of self-aggrandizement.

These thoughts are active in our minds, and as situations arise which require direction it is these ideas which are invoked, and they subtly shape our decisions. Our character is formed by the environment of ideas which inhabit our minds.

We are the product of our thoughts. Let a man condition himself to think nobly, heroically. So will he act. So will he be.

More than Skin-Deep

'Save the surface and you save all.' This slogan was once coined by an advertising executive for a nationally known paint manufacturer. No greater lie has ever been placed on the billboards.

The surface is important. It is the first impression to be registered by the eye. But reality runs deeper than the surface, and the eye's first impressions are often deceptive or incomplete. Many a beautiful apple contains a worm.

Many a well-polished automobile has a defective motor. It is easy to give the surface a new coat of paint, but we labor in vain if the concealed interior is rotten.

That advertising man capitalized on a common human weakness of going by the eye's first impressions. We judge people by their exterior, their appearance, their manners, their clothes. Witness, for example, the widely ramified cosmetics industry, which specializes in appearances. If you add up what the nation spends on clothes, you are approaching an annual budget that may be greater than our national debt.

Outward appearances are important, but what about the inner person? If our outlook on life is warped, if we are mean and irritable, if we are given to fits of temper, to brooding over trifles, then we are disqualified from a happy adjustment to life. If our mind is bare or overgrown with the weeds of inane and foolish ideas, then exterior elegance will not save us. In a time of testing, our weakness will show through and we will give way under the strain.

The surface is part of life, but it is not all of it. Look beneath it to discover its intrinsic condition. By all means give the surface its due, but see that your elegance is more than skin-deep.

Rotate Your Ideas

Every farmer who considers his soil knows he must plant his crop in rotation. A soil in which you continue to grow one crop, whether cabbage or cotton, will before long become depleted, because different substances are used up for every crop it produces. It must call on special energies to fertilize the seed to push it up from its inner chambers in the earth towards the sun, and to nurture the tender plant till harvest time. And when year after year, the earth is forced to labor without respite or variation it becomes devitalized.

The salvation of the soil is in allowing it to rest, so that it may recuperate its energies. It is achieved, above all, by rotating crops. The periodic change from one crop to another saves the soil from monotony, and enables it to maintain a more productive life.

The human mind is like that farmer's soil. If you continue to think the same thoughts, to concentrate on the same kind of problem, mental anaemia will set in. You will become mentally dull – to yourself and to the world.

Mental vigour depends on rotating your ideas. By taking your mind off your customary routine, and allowing yourself to pursue other interests, you will enjoy the benefits of a change. You will be stimulated and you will achieve a more balanced and therefore a happier life.

Honeyed Words

Men love honeyed words, but these are not without their danger. We like such words, because they proclaim our excellence, and reassure us as to our worth. But in every person there are elements of imperfection and praise, offered in undue measure, may lull us into a smug acceptance of ourselves, blunting the sense of our deficiency, so that we cease striving to do better, to be better.

Honest praise must always be accompanied by some criticism. A parent who never applies the rod will spoil the child. A friend who will not occasionally administer a word of reproof has failed in one of the important kindnesses which friends can render each other. A nation that is not occasionally challenged, by the ringing voice of critics, to lay bare its weaknesses, is without the leaven that enables it to rise to greater heights.

The most beautiful shapes wrought by a goldsmith, are achieved by hammering. Each stroke administered brings closer the transformation from amorphous matter to the thing of beauty envisaged in his design.

Lazy minds don't want to be hammered, and this is why some men dislike criticism. But woe unto such lazy minds, who are their own worst enemies. We move towards greater perfection not by means of the honeyed words of 'yes-men,' but through the rebuke of the honest critic who prods us into overcoming our imperfections.

A Wider Vision

Mary was young and beautiful, and she was in love with herself. Like some artist working in clay to fashion an object of perfect beauty, she worked on her own body. She followed all the rules....she exercised; she dieted; she used the most expensive creams for her hands and face; she tinted her hair with never-failing regularity. She was determined to add, to what the Lord had given her, the sparkle of her own perfect grooming. Yet she remained deeply dissatisfied. Before the scrutiny of her critical eye, she was never flawless.

One night she had a strange dream. She saw herself living in a room completely surrounded by mirrors; wherever she turned she was able to see herself perfectly. Every crease in her dress, a speck of dust, a hair, was at once revealed to her. And she was able to study her posture, when she sat, when she stood, when she walked. The world was completely shut out, and she was able to concentrate on herself.

At first she was quite happy with the arrangement, yet before long she began to weary of it. And once weariness set in, it grew more unbearable by the minute. She somehow suspected that it was only a dream but she could not awaken.

Then she heard herself shriek, and grabbing a stone she threw it at the mirror. And lo and behold, when the mirror crashed into pieces, she was startled to find in the open space a clear view of the world outside. She saw the skyline of the city, and the streets teeming with life. The view thrilled her beyond words and she gasped with the joy of it.

Then taking more stones she threw them at the rest of the mirrors. At the sound of the crashing glass, she awoke. For the rest of the night she lay sleepless, meditating on her strange experience. 'Perhaps,' she finally said to herself, 'this is exactly what I need. I must break my mirrors. My eyes are tired of seeing the self-same image, the image of my own ego. They crave to see the larger world.'

The Test of Idleness

There are many conditions that test a man, but among the most searching is idleness. A demanding routine can be borne by almost any man. But only people of great intellectual and moral strength can bear idleness.

The idle moment releases the heart and mind from

external affairs. It forces a man to face inwards, to confront himself. It is in idle moments that we reflect on the meaning of our busy days, and evaluate our goals. It is in such moments that the hushed voice of conscience speaks more audibly, and seeks to bring us into harmony with the basic laws of the universe. These laws are God's laws, and the voice of conscience is God's accompanying whisper, reminding us of our true destination whenever we have gone astray.

Many people dare not confront themselves, and so they cannot bear idleness. They must fill in every moment with activity. When purposeful activity is not at hand, they will resort to artificial activity to keep busy. With nowhere to go, they will still drive madly on the highway of life. This activity for activity's sake is a means of avoiding reflection. It is the loud noise we generate to drown out the pressing demands of a troubled conscience.

Happy is the man who finds joy in work and peace in idleness.

A Balanced Life

We pay a price for everything. And the gains we make in every phase of our advancement are not without some balancing liabilities.

We have often praised the man who has the power to concentrate. It is a great accomplishment, but it is often achieved at a considerable cost, to that man and to his world.

This capacity of a person to direct all his energies towards a given task tends to withdraw him from something else. The mother who listens with rapt attention to the music

from the radio has, by the same token, become less atten-
tive to the baby in the other room, or the soup that is
cooking on the stove.

The price of withdrawal by which we buy the power
of concentration is made glaringly evident in the fields of
cultural specialization. One great scientist confessed recently
that during the years prior to the Second World War, he
was so engrossed in the problems of theoretical physics
that he did not read a newspaper. His labors yielded a
rich reward. He was one of the pioneers in the development
of atomic energy, but he paid a price in a diminished
attentiveness to his duties as a citizen. Artists, poets, dreamers
of all kinds, have often been oblivious of the world and
its problems, precisely because they concentrated on their
visions. And business men have often been impatient with
any other dimension of living, because they have committed all their energies to the world of practical affairs.

Let us beware of the perils of concentration and specialization. As the diver returns periodically from the lower
depths to refill his lungs with fresh air, so must we ever
return to the broad surface of the world if we are to maintain
a balanced and many-sided life.

A Question of Perspective

A new elevator attendant had been engaged for the library
building of the University, to be on duty in the late after-
noon and evening. John who had the day shift, greeted
him warmly when he first met him, but he noticed a
certain reserve in the man. He wondered why.

After they became better acquainted, the new elevator
man became more confidential. He was clearly disgruntled

with his job. 'All I do is press buttons and open and close doors,' he said. 'I feel as though I am wasting my life. I wonder how you have stood it here for all these years,' he continued, looking at his colleague who was now also his friend.

John smiled, and after some hesitation replied: 'My job is more exciting. I am a partner of all these scholars who come into this building. I am an aid to their labors. Does not a journey round the world begin with a single step? I like to think that some of my work, no matter how small, is represented in the study and research which go on here. For me, this is glory enough.'

Unclaimed Assets

Banks occasionally advertise unclaimed assets. Deposits of substantial sums have been forgotten by their owners, and over a period of many years those funds have increased. How many pressing needs could those funds meet, if their owners were only conscious of their existence?

As I watch life, I am impressed with the fact that the tragedy of unclaimed assets is not confined to bank deposits. People often feel a deep need for the resources of living. They crave friendship. They would like the thrill of creative work. They would like the opportunity to serve in some worthy cause for human betterment. But they are oppressed with the thought that they lack the aptitude necessary for such accomplishment. But how very many of these people really do have sufficient aptitude, yet fail to claim it?

Have you ever noticed what tenderness people show one another in time of illness? In the face of threatening tragedy members of a family will get together and strive with boundless energy and patience for a given end. In time of war, the nation rises above its factions and acts with unity to meet the crisis. To what extent are these resources for living drawn upon in times when the challenge is not so formidable? We often crave these resources in normal times as well, but we are not aware that we possess them. Below the parched dry land, underground springs of living water flow undetected.

Next time you withdraw from some deeply felt desire because you lack the power to pursue it, re-examine your life. Deep within it, in some underground channel, a spring of living water may be waiting to be tapped.

Many a man is richer than he thinks. His problem is to take command of his assets.

We Discard Polluting Elements

I am grateful for my ability to remember, for without it my life would be a series of meaningless sensations. But I am equally grateful that I have the ability to forget.

What would my life be if all my past experiences were actively at work in my consciousness? Some of my past deeds were foolish and would annoy me. Others were more than foolish; they were the errors over which I stumbled. I have since outgrown them, and recalling them would only bring me renewed humiliation. And there have been griefs, hurts, frustrations, which I had to accept, and they are shadows which still haunt me now and then. But if they were always before me, my life would be darkened with an unbearable melancholy. I can live because I can forget.

A river cleans itself as it flows along. Polluting elements

are eliminated when they drop to the bottom. A healthy mind works similarly. It drops polluting elements to the subconscious.

Woe unto the person whose mechanism for forgetting breaks down! He who cannot forget has disqualified himself for life no less than he who cannot remember.

Life's Larger Goals

One woman says: 'I am scrubbing the floor.' Another woman says: 'I am cleaning my home.' Both describe an identical performance. But the difference between their descriptions reveals a momentous difference between their respective outlooks on life.

Every human activity has a higher and lower meaning. Its lower meaning consists in seeing it only for what it is, without reference to larger purposes. Almost all work is drab and insignificant when seen as an isolated enterprise, detached from life's greater goals.

Who can possibly enjoy scrubbing floors? Who can enjoy shopping and cooking and doing the dishes when the meal is done? Who can enjoy fussing with an infant barely able to perform the most elemental functions alone? The work in the office or factory is no different. There is no glamor in making buttons all day or in selling shoes, or slip covers or soda pop. No individual act is particularly inspiring, until we see it as part of a greater goal.

The woman who can see her household duties as incidental to the welfare of her family will not rebel at any task however menial it seems. In the same way, your work in office or factory, even if not particularly exciting, will take on greater meaning if you think of it in a larger context, as a service you are rendering towards some larger human need.

A scientist will engage in the most trivial work in the course of his research. He will study a cell under the microscope. He will assess the behavior of a rat. He will calculate the momentum of a penny falling from a height. He will expose himself to the frigid wastes of the North Pole as well as to the steaming jungles of the tropics. What relieves the trial and tedium of these proceedings? His search – the search for a larger objective. Whatever will help him attain that objective ceases to be trivial and becomes of great importance.

Life is a complex endeavor, consisting of many individual enterprises, significant only in their contribution to a larger whole. Work by the light of life's greater goals. It will lift every act to the plane of high significance.

Relative Contentment

Contentment must be relative. Perfect contentment would reconcile a man to his condition in the world, and make him accept his circumstances with finality, even resignation. But no set of circumstances represents the limit of our possibilities. Whatever we may be – there lies something beyond, which is closer to the ideal. A person must therefore accept himself with some reservation, to make himself ever capable of change.

On the other hand, the beckoning visions of what we lack must not blind us to the virtues of what we have. Our attainments, our resources and abilities, may not be perfect, but they represent some of the assets for living. To draw upon them freely, and joyously, is the task of today.

Tomorrow, another sunset will light up the horizon with, perhaps, richer colours than I now see. My eyes must be ready for that new beauty, but I must know how to find contentment in the partial beauty which this moment offers me.

A Tragic Distortion

The newspapers reported a recent suicide of a young college girl. In a note which she left to her family she said, among other things: 'There isn't enough life in me to sustain me through the long years ahead.'

What a tragic mental distortion is revealed in this note! This young lady assumed that there is in us a fixed supply of that something called life from which we continue to draw, from day to day, from year to year. No wonder she was obsessed with a fear of insufficiency. No one has enough in him or her at any one time to sustain him through the years ahead. As the waters of a spring keep on being renewed however much we draw on them, so is life renewed for us, in the course of living it. The question is only whether there is enough life in us to sustain us for this one hour and its needs. The next hour will beget other needs, but the Giver of life will renew our strength as He will renew our life for the hour ahead.

A good deal of the grief which agitates people derives from the same mental distortion of weighing the total sum of life's possible demands against the visible assets of any one hour. This is why they are often consumed with worry. They feel a lack of physical and mental resources for life's long duration. We were meant to take life in stages of more manageable proportions. If there are resources enough for the time at hand, it is for us to draw on them confidently. He Who sets the time of life will also give us the resources with which to live it.

Once a young man facing marriage was overcome with anxiety. Where would he get the words and thoughts to maintain conversation with his beloved during the long years ahead? This question was to him a source of endless grief, until he unburdened himself to his mother. She gave him the reassuring answer: Words and thoughts come to us as we need them. They are not stocked up in static quantities.

The fountain of life continues to well up in an ever-renewing bounty. Take into your cup enough for today's needs. There will be fresh water for your cup tomorrow.

Self-Confidence

Psychologists have often preached to us the need for self-confidence. But what can sustain us in feeling self-confident? It is not the person who lives by the illusion that he is all-powerful who needs this advice, but he who is conscious of his inadequacies. What can help us overcome the feeling of inadequacy and enable us to meet life with confidence?

One thing is clear – confidence requires a more sturdy support than the resources possessed by the self. Is there anyone who, seeing himself in true perspective, can say: 'I am equal to whatever will confront me'? If all I could draw upon were the resources at present in my possession, I would be bound to feel unequal to life's impending encounters. Countless are the people who fear to face the march of life because they feel inadequate.

We can be rescued from the feeling of inadequacy by realizing that the inexhaustible source of power which resides in God is available to reinforce our own efforts. All we have to do is plug in on the reservoir of divine energy, and power will come flowing into our own lives. Strength is not in the muscle, which is only the obedient tool of the spirit, and the spirit is strong only when it is in contact with the eternal spirit, in Whom is inexhaustible strength.

Confidence is one of life's most precious assets. But the self cannot be an ultimate basis for it. Self-confidence can derive only from confidence in God.

The Uses of a Guilty Conscience

Men have occasionally idealized the virtue of untroubled conscience, yet there is nothing more dangerous to the soul.

Only a person who is completely satisfied with himself can have a clear conscience, and this no man has a right to, for no human life is without blemish.

We do not have to commit an act of flagrant wrongdoing to be troubled by a sense of guilt. The path of shortcoming and imperfection is often subtly hidden from the human heart, but we all trod upon this path at one time or another in our lives. For who can ever fulfill every possible moral obligation? Who can say that he has given his children just the right amount of love? Who can say that he has acted towards his fellow human beings with the right amount of compassion and understanding? Who can say that he has pursued truth, justice, and peace with sufficient fervour? Who can say that he has always shown goodness its due reverence?

The realm of possible goodness is infinite, and man can never attain it. His condition must therefore be one of permanent frustration or, in the vocabulary of religion, of continual sinfulness. This is not meant to induce in us a sense of pessimism about the future of man. Man is forever frustrated only because he seeks the absolute, the unattainable. It is no dishonor to fail, for in the quest itself is glory enough, and honor exists in the partial success which crowns our strivings.

The person who thinks himself wholly commendable is using an inadequate yardstick of judgment, and his blindness will necessarily make him self-righteous. He will lose what a person needs most – an unending sense of insufficiency to inspire a continual feeling of need for purging, for repentance, for improvement.

It is irritating to have a guilty conscience. But only the people who are irritated with things as they are will carry themselves – and their world – towards nobler heights.

Climbing Through Descent

Fortunate at times are the sinners. Grand are the possibilities open to them, for no greater momentum to moral striving is at a man's disposal than the power generated by renouncing sin. A diver needs a platform sufficiently firm from which to dive. The sinner's situation, when admitted, offers a firm basis from which to strike out in the direction of goodness.

Energy is generated through a clash of opposites. The power needed for significant moral and spiritual advance is often generated out of the clash between good and evil.

The successful encounter with evil releases a tide that carries us along on its way. The static goodness of people who have never been tempted is often without force, without resilience, without meaning. The sinner who has repented his sin occupies holier ground than the saint whose saintliness has never been put to the test. To err is human, but the act of renouncing error brings us closer to the divine.

By descending from a height, mountain climbers will occasionally secure a surer grip on the earth under their feet and so make a loftier climb possible. A variety of paths lead us towards God, including the path which ostensibly appears to take us away from Him. Sometimes our depravities are also our opportunities.

True Heirs

The living grieve for the dead, and sometimes their grief is inconsolable. They grieve not only for those who are gone, but for themselves as well. For the danger of friendship and of love is that we become part of those we love, and when they perish, part of us perishes with them.

But is there not consolation also in this, for if we become part of them, are they not also part of us? And if something of ourselves dies with those who have died, does not something of them remain living with the living?

Grief engendered by the loss of a loved one is natural enough. But inconsolable grief is an injustice to the dead no less than to the living. For we remain the means ot resurrection and immortality for those we love. The part of them which remains living in us demands a fuller and more vital life. They who refuse to be consoled in their grief and shun the call of continuing life consign those for whom they grieve to a second death.

Every person who truly grieves for one who has died becomes his heir. And the chief inheritance which is left to him is the mandate to go on living.

Love Yourself

Moralists have written an extensive literature about the need to love our neighbours. But is it not just as important to be reminded of the prior duty of loving ourselves?

Love is an emotion expressing itself in a favourable disposition towards the beloved. When we love someone we treat him kindly, we overlook his shortcomings and judge him favorably, we think of him as a person of dignity and value, we believe in his capacities to grow towards ever greater perfection in the mastery of his powers and in utilizing them towards worth-while ends.

Is there not as widespread a violation of self-love, as there is of the love we owe towards others? There are many people who never learned to be kind to themselves. They refuse to overlook their shortcomings, and they judge themselves unfavorably. They continue to speak ill of themselves. They are destructive in their self-criticism, and portray themselves as mean and unworthy people, as failures and as scoundrels. They resent themselves as bitterly as a man may resent anyone who has incurred his disfavor.

Hatred is a poison that engenders physical as well as emotional illness, and as deadly when directed against one's self as it is when directed against others. If hatred is intense enough, it will drive people to rash acts. When directed at others, it has driven people to commit murder. When directed at one's self, it has on occasion also inspired self-murder, or suicide. Multitudes of people go about the world embittered by feuds against their fellow humans. And there are multitudes who carry on these feuds with themselves. They are split personalities, one part of them locked in deadly conflict with another part.

We may love different people in different ways. But a person with an open heart and generous spirit will find something lovable in every one of God's creatures. In each of them is embodied some spark of the divine, and they are all worthy of our solicitude and our love.

But is not that divine spark present in ourselves also? Is there not something lovable in us too? We need to respect our own dignity and worth. We need to think well of ourselves, to believe in our own powers and potentialities. Kindness, like charity, must not end at home, but it should always begin there.

The law of love is all-inclusive in its dominion. We must love ourselves even as we must love our neighbors.

Togetherness

The sturdiest power we meet in life is the earth itself. It carries the total load of the world's existence. Yet the earth consists ultimately of single grains of matter. Each grain standing alone would be feeble. Each, joined in its strength to others, converts weakness into formidable might.

We men and women of the world have been fashioned by God as single, unique individuals. The fulfillment of our lives depends in part on our playing the role of the unique individual. We must know how to follow the bent of our minds, to stand alone, to follow our own path amid the divergent pathways of living. But there is another dimension to our being. We must also know the art of forgetting our private world, to step out of it and to join our strength to the strength of other men in pursuit of common goals.

A nation, a business, household, a family group, a religious community – their achievements depend among other things on this capacity of men to rise from single grains into compact wholes. A house divided is a feeble house. A house can be strong when those who live in it know, when the occasion demands it, to be together, to think and feel and act as one.

A society that knows only the virtue of togetherness will end up as a society of slaves. But a society that knows only the virtue of each man's privacy will be atomized to a point of impotence.

Two Extremes

We have often decried the tendency of people to limit the things they value to their own circle of life. There are some to whom the word 'foreign' spells at once something objectionable. Only their particular friends, only their city, their country, only their religious or social community embodies what is worthwhile. Those outside this charmed circle are deemed as of relatively lesser worth. This weakness of human nature has often been diagnosed under the name of provincialism and the world has been duly warned against it.

There is, however, another weakness in our natures

which represents the opposite extreme. We may label it as self-baiting. There are some people who always idealize what someone else has and disparage their own. Someone else's grass is always greener. The neighbor's car, job, house, clothes, children, friends are always more attractive, and in comparison we feel inferior. In certain circles an imported article is always preferable to the home product. For a long time American intellectuals sneered at their own country's culture and always held up Europe's achievements as best.

Why do some of us wait to reach foreign shores and then trek through the interesting sights, the museums, the buildings of historical interest, while we neglect comparable sights at home? Why do some people go seeking at alien tables the bread of faith to nourish their souls when an ample store is waiting for them in their own household?

Both extremes are bad – the repudiation of the unfamiliar as well as an over-fascination with it. We should see the world with sober eyes and cherish what is good wherever it appears to us. And the place to begin is – home.

NOT A SELF-MADE MAN

I did not make the air I breathe,
Nor the sun that warms me.
I did not place in the seed
The secret
That bears my bounty.
I did not endow the muscles
Of hand and brain

With the strength
To plough and plant and harvest.
My harvest
Is also His harvest.
I know
I am not
A self-made man.

The Measure of Man

EVERY creative act of man is a fusion between the infinite and the finite. The ideas which inspire us are sparks of the divine fire, scattered fragments of God's own truth. They are beyond perfect realization by mortal man.

The laws we pass cannot give us perfect justice, the music we play is but an imperfect rendering of the vision which inspired the composer, the perfect house has never been constructed, the perfect sermon has never been preached. All creators struggle to express a vision, which is always bigger than their power of expression. The product that finally emerges from their efforts is an imperfect interpretation of a vision that always remains elusive to the human powers of expression.

A truly creative person therefore will always feel some misgiving about his work, for even when the world applauds, he will remain humbled by the knowledge of the truth and the beauty which eluded him.

Those who have never tasted the joy as well as the frustration of a truly creative act may be irritated when they discover that the work of some master is marred by an imperfection. If they have bought such work at some public counter they may even feel cheated. They are vexed because they have not appreciated the true measure of man. Man can only glimpse at the truth and offer an imperfect interpretation of it. He cannot ever capture it whole.

We should not be vexed that perfection eludes us. It is because perfection is elusive that life remains an unending quest, forever exciting with emergent potential.

This Is Man

Man has often been challenged to know himself, but this is an extremely difficult task. We are too close to the scene of our lives to be able to see ourselves in true perspective. No man can know a mountain when he stands on its peak. Only when he gains distance from his object can he secure a faithful view.

The quest for self-knowledge is difficult too, because there is no static self upon which we focus our gaze: man is always in flux. New circumstances bring out new powers; new encounters propel us in new directions. Occasionally some vision of good to be done, or beauty to be fashioned, appears on our horizon and we become uplifted by a new dedication, informed with new purpose. Out of the pain of brooding over some problem crying for redress, we suddenly yield to the persistent whisper calling us to service. Or some mad passion possesses us and we break under its impact.

Man is always in a process of becoming, and any fixed image of him is bound to be false.

We can know ourselves only as we look in the mirror of the past, and in that of the future. We can look in the mirror of the past by remembering man's slow ascent out of his primeval condition, and in that of the future by recollecting the visions and hopes and dreams towards whose fulfillment men of all times have aspired in spite of the perils of earthly existence.

Man stands between these two worlds, yesterday's and tomorrow's. The navel cord attaching him to the past, to the time before his birth, is not fully cut; tomorrow's world he can see only by the light of faith, and that dimly. The spirit calls him to go forward but it is hard to scale the heights, and he hesitates. Occasionally he climbs ahead but slips and falls back. And then he tries once more.

This is man – a pilgrim in time – climbing, sometimes trudging, on toward the peaks of a world not yet born, but partly of his own making, following a call that summons him onward.

Man and God

Is man made in God's image? In believing this to be so, are we accepting the notion that God is endowed with a bodily structure, that He is man-like in appearance.

Many have stumbled grievously over this question. The difficulty has arisen from a misinterpretation of the term 'image.' Man's image is not his physical frame, but that which makes him human, which raises him above the rest of the animal kingdom.

The distinguishing mark of man is the fact that in addition to his physical self, with its natural instincts, man also possesses a spiritual self which prompts him to higher pursuits. It is his soul, his intellect which prompts him to create, to dream, to think. It prompts him to seek beauty and truth and goodness. It prompts him to seek friendship and peace, with others, and when necessary to strike out on an independent path, following new visions which appear on his personal horizon.

When we declare that man is made in God's image, we mean that man's soul, his intellect, offers us an echo of the divine presence. There is a vast difference between man's mind and the divine mind, between man's soul and the divine soul. But the essence remains the same; fire is fire, and mind is mind, soul is soul.

God is not a physical body, and He is without a tangible presence. But God whose essence is a mystery that eludes us, conferred upon man a great distinction. Into his physical frame, He implanted a spark of the holy fire, He endowed him with a soul, a mind by which he can rise above his frame of dust and soar towards the heights.

The Feat of the Mountaineers

So man has conquered Mount Everest and the Himalayas! Why has the ascent to these great summits continued to intrigue people through the generations? It is because the forbidding height has been a symbol of man's own limits. Thus far he has been able to go, but no farther, no higher. And the human spirit which does not lightly yield to imposed limitations, has pitted its ingenuity and skill against the heights.

A forbidding height scaled is a victory not for the individual climber alone, but for all men. It is a victory for the human spirit, for its daring, its perseverance, its fascination with the challenge, its readiness to risk all in order to extend man's sovereignty over his world.

But there is a sobering afterthought to these exultations

over victory. Has man really conquered those heights? For a land is only conquered when you can make it your own, and all that man has done is to peep at these hidden worlds on high. For a fleeting moment his feet stood at the top and he looked down. Amidst the snow drifts and fog and ice, the man on the summit remains a puny figure, a symbol of helplessness.

Mount Everest and Annapurna have been invaded for a moment, but the invader was soon forced to retreat, bruised and beaten, and often maimed for having dared the attempt. Those summits remain defiant, towering towards the sky, in their proud isolation, above the world of mortal men.

The human spirit was meant to be daring, to pit itself against formidable tasks, but man must accept with resignation the fact that there are limits beyond which he cannot prevail. He can extend those limits, he can push the boundary into realms previously denied him, but there is always a boundary. Man's hands cannot grasp the whole of creation.

The feats of the mountaineers confirm both elements in man, his greatness as well as his limitations.

Weakness Makes Us Human

Weakness contributes to our well-being just as strength does. If our children were so strong that they did not need or want our help, we would be unable to do anything for them. Thus would be destroyed one of the elements which makes for endearment between parents and children.

If a wife, a husband, a friend, were so strong that each was self-sufficient and one could not do anything for the other, one of the elements which deepen a tender human relationship would be dissolved.

The pet we tend lovingly, the flowers we cultivate, offer us these opportunities of lavishing care, because of a quality of weakness. If they could thrive without our care, we would be denied a precious opportunity of expressing affection.

A world without weakness would be a world in which men would not need to turn to God for courage and comfort, for the strength to meet the commitments of living.

A world without weakness would be a world without compassion. For we can be compassionate only towards the weak, who need us. A world without weakness would be a world in which each creature possessed vastly increased powers, but it would be a cold and merciless world, without sympathy, without humanity. The warmest human feelings would die out in such a world, withering through disuse.

Thank God for weakness. It helps to keep us human.

Gambling

The gambler has usually been disparaged by society. Yet gambling is a necessary expression of human nature.

A gamble is a venture into the unknown, by anticipating results before they have transpired. When people decide to marry they are taking a chance with their lives, since they don't know how their marriage will work out. That is a gamble. When we enter a profession or go into business, we are taking a risk. We are, in other words, gambling. So did every prophet, every social reformer, every pioneer in any realm of life, for they committed their energies in the hope that their vision was capable of realization and that men would follow their call to make the dream come true.

We cannot ever lift the curtain which divides the present from the future, but the human spirit always dares to conjecture what lies beyond. Is not religious faith a gamble, too, for the very highest stakes imaginable? For it rests on a vision that there is a God in this world, who governs His creatures in righteousness and in love, and that man was meant to be His co-worker, His partner, in the unending labors of creation.

Every gambler is a man of faith. The difference is only on what we gamble, in what we place our faith. Some men place their faith in God, in the eventual triumph of righteousness over evil, and they act on the assumption that the future will vindicate their faith. Others place their faith on a horse...or the shuffling of a pack of cards.

The cynic is also a man of faith. He does not really know that ideals are false, but he stakes his life on the faith that this is so. In the name of his faith, he mocks men who believe in a different order of values. The boldest venture of faith is atheism itself – summoning us to live on the faith that there is no God.

But we cannot live merely by what we know. At best, we know only the moment and that slips out of our hands before we can act. Life faces the unknown and when we face the unknown, we must take chances, based on faith.

On what shall we place our faith? This is life's most challenging question. And our entire life is only an elaboration of our reply.

The Child and the Dog

My eight year old son finally had his way. He received a dog for his birthday. Why are pets so precious to a child, or to a grown-up for that matter? Because they respond to the common human need to love and be loved.

A child enjoys the love of his parents, and he can offer love in return, but that love is not unqualified. The parent will often be stern and impose discipline. That discipline is, of course, inspired by love but the child cannot always understand this. The dog's love, being free from the wish to educate, is without moments of bitterness, and therefore appears to the child as more wholehearted.

A child can love his parents in return, but his parents seem to him independent of his love. He is not strong enough to contribute materially to their needs, and what he can contribute seems to him too trivial to be significant. The dog, on the other hand, greatly values the minor bounties of which a child is capable.

In the tender love between the child and the dog, I see a clue to a fundamental fact about our natures. We all need to love and to be loved.

All Men Are Different

It has been said that the basis of freedom is the belief that all men were created equal. This belief rests on a false premise. There are no duplicates in God's universe. All His creatures are original creations, and they all differ from each other in some special way. Even flakes of snow show different designs under the microscope, and people are likewise differentiated in body and in mind.

A world in which all men were treated equally would not be a free world. We cannot each live by the same quantity or quality of food; we can't each be content with the same style of life or the same conditions of work, or the same kind of education. A world where all men were treated with mathematical equality would be the essence of regimentation, which is not freedom, but tyranny.

Freedom rests on the recognition that all men are created different.

We can say that every man has a unique offering for the world in his own personality. His life is therefore one of the irreplaceable assets of the universe.

Men are equal only in the sense that they are all equally unique, equally different. And a free world is one where each person is enabled fully to develop his unique, distinctive self, and to express that self in an unimpeded exchange with his fellow men. To each we must give in accordance with his needs and from each we have a right to expect a return in accordance with his capacities.

Passage to Maturity

Have you ever tasted an unripe apple? And do you remember how you at once thrust it aside because it was sour to the taste? All living things are like that. They do not attain their true qualities until they are fully grown. The basic problem which confronts any living being is to grow up, to ripen, to pass into maturity.

The maturity of some living things is simple to attain. The apple will ripen automatically, provided it is allowed to remain on the tree sufficiently long, but on the human level, an act of will is required. We are free creatures who are privileged to participate in the shaping of our lives. The habits developed during childhood do not automatically cease as we grow in years, and we must free ourselves from their sway by an act of conscious will and occasionally of fierce struggle, otherwise we will be haunted by a lingering childishness.

What is the difference between the child and the mature person? The differences are many but they all stem from the manner of meeting the strenuous facts of living.

A child evades responsibility by the simple response: 'I can't.' And how many adults have answered the call to some task with the same excuse? They give this excuse to others, and they give it to themselves, as well, to silence a demanding conscience. They may even reinforce their excuse with an assumption of illness. A good deal of the world's mental, emotional, and even physical illness has its origin in the wish to evade a disagreeable duty. The body and the mind obey our deep felt wishes, and shield us from the harsh facts of life; they will even veil from us the true source of our illness.

A child needs these defenses because his tender ego must be protected from the severe pressures of harsh circumstance. But is it not tragic to find an adult obsessed with them as well? It takes courage to grow up, fearlessly to face one's self and one's world. But we are bound to this act of courage by the very privilege which has been conferred on us, of being creatures capable of free will and free decision.

Unlike the apple which ripens automatically in response to environmental factors, we must exercise our own free initiative in passing to maturity.

Let every person act as befits his age. Let his maturity

match his years. Only then will he come into full possession of his strength and play his destined role as a citizen of the world.

Each Day Counts

'How long did it take you to paint this picture?' an admirer asked the artist. The artist hesitated, and thinking of his next birthday, replied: 'Thirty-six years.'

The artist was right. The time of painting that picture could not be reckoned by the days he spent in putting brush and paint to canvas. Every past experience was part of it. His sense of beauty, his delicacy of perception, his ability to subdue every distraction to the creative dedication, were developed in him by all the years of his life. Every past canvas he had done had helped train his hand for his present work.

We live at any one moment with our total past. We hate with all our past hatreds. We love with all our past loves. Every sunset we have ever seen has formed our sense of the beautiful. Every bar of music we have listened to is included in our response to the melody which now rings in our ears.

This is why it is so important that we be cautious in what we make of each day. It will stay with us always.

Daily Bread

The sources of the energy that sustains our lives must be replenished periodically. They do not come as a permanent treasure that can be possessed once and for all, and then be inexhaustibly drawn on, when and as required. This is why we need daily bread. The living body rapidly uses up its intake, and if life is to go on, the nourishment must be continually replenished.

The life of the spirit, too, needs continual nourishment. The bread of vision and faith that sustains it suffices only for a limited time. It is used up in the course of living, and there must be renewal if we are not to suffer spiritual anaemia.

Many people are afflicted with a pernicious spiritual anaemia without being aware of it. Their bodies are well upholstered, but the spirit that animates the body with will and purpose, is often feeble and inept. Listless, apathetic, indifferent – they are like uncharged batteries. They find life a weary business, because they are without the vital energy with which the spirit generates the momentum and direction for living.

We renew the spirit's nourishment in moments of prayer, when we establish contact with God Who is the source of the will and purpose which permeates the life of the universe. We nourish the spirit when we enjoy fellowship with other men and women, whose spirits are well charged with the vital energies of life. Every experience of beauty and goodness yields a store of energy to strengthen us. The books we read, the people we associate with, the entertainment we enjoy – these are foodstuffs of the spirit, and they must be taken regularly as part of the continual rhythm of living.

Dignity and Duty

Man is the most distinguished citizen in God's world, but he is not without his deficiencies. Mortal creatures are bound to be imperfect, in body as in mind. When we contemplate the unending mystery of existence and the more baffling mystery of its Creator, we are overcome with a sense of profound humility.

But our humility does not negate our greatness. Alone among all God's earthly creatures, we have the urge to attain the knowledge which, however murky, has been a window open to the mystery of the universe. Man with his microscope and telescopes, looking with the body's eyes and the mind's, has discovered secrets of great wonder about the tiniest organism and the vastest world in space. And man, alone among all other creatures, has heard The Voice speak to him from the very midst of the wonders of existence. Messages of illumination and inspiration have poured in upon him which he has translated into the beauty of words and pictures.

And because such great distinction has been conferred upon man, he faces an equally great responsibility. From all the worlds of God's creation, a music of great harmony continues to rise towards their Creator. And man must play the music of his own world, using the abounding potentialities of his hand and heart and mind as his instruments. He must join in the great symphony with all his fellow creatures to create a harmonious whole. It is a challenging task, but can we accept our dignity while shunning our duty?

Praised be the man who is a good citizen in God's universe. He justifies the work of his Creator.

An Unending Dialogue

Life is an unending dialogue. The world continues to speak to us what is in its mind. It speaks to us through people, and through things, all of which make some impression on us. And we react to the world, expressing what is in our minds and in our hearts.

There are times when this dialogue breaks down. The world may refuse to listen to us, or we to the world. Many a man has come with great riches, ready to offer them as his gift to humanity, but the world has refused to hear him. It has ordered him instead to be silent. This enforced silence is the greatest indignity, and like every spurned love, it causes a frustration that cuts to the very soul.

There are also times when a man refuses to listen to the world. Smugly content with his own life, he builds a barricade about himself to keep everybody else out. His life is a boring monologue, repeating the self-same tune, never allowing another melody to be played in his ears. Such a man has doomed himself to suffer spiritual impoverishment.

The world is free when the dialogue is unimpeded, when no man is excluded by society or by his own voluntary withdrawal from this mutual give and take of the mind.

The Arrogant Mind

The arrogant mind is fed by the false illusion of man's self-sufficiency. The person who recognizes his limitations will necessarily feel humble about himself and, ever eager to broaden his point of view, will reach out with sympathy and gratitude towards new truths, regardless of their source. On the other hand, he who lives by the illusion of his own sufficiency will close his mind to the world, remaining hostile towards those who bring him new ideas, since he regards his own truth, his own life, as complete, without need of amplification.

The arrogant are guilty of the idolatry of self-worship. It is only God who is beyond the need of amplification, because only He is self-sufficient, only He is perfect. And when men presume to be possessors of the full truth, to be complete and self-sufficient beings, they arrogate to themselves the characteristics belonging to God.

The arrogant man will be puffed up with pride and exalt himself over his fellow creatures. He may make an impressive external show, but his life will be barren.

The mountains make a grand appearance, but they are rocky and unproductive. They cannot retain the water which alone nourishes life, and sustains new growth. Water settles in the valley. It is the lowlands which yield the greatest bounty for mankind.

Give Them Sustenance

The plants in my garden are still undistinguishable in the uniformity of their green. They will become individually striking when they begin to blossom. Then each will appear in the distinctive glory of its own beauty, yielding the harvest of color and fragrance which is its mission to the world.

I have often reflected on this transformation in my plants which takes place within a brief span of days. It takes of course more than just days. It also takes the proper cultivation – scattering plant food, weeding, watering, and also the energies latent in earth, and sun, and the caressing breezes that blow – to enable my plants to grow to the fullness of their promise.

I have reflected on this process because it offers so keen an insight into the human condition as well. Individuals go through a like transformation. Peoples and nations also often present themselves to us as undistinguished. No richness of creation or culture is to be seen in their lives. And we sometimes say: 'They are uncreative.' But may it not be that we see them before their full span of development has revealed the beauty still sleeping in their souls?

People are like plants in requiring proper cultivation to bring into being the promise inherent in their lives. They need food and shelter, and the warmth of affection; their minds need educating and stimulating by the challenge of other minds in action. Without proper sustenance, plants die green, and so do people.

True Healers

The dough is bulky, but it stays flat until a small proportion of leaven is added to it. This is the story of civilization.

The multitudes of humanity are contented to stay flat. They are content to remain in their stagnant condition, suffering whatever evils beset them. Their powers of endurance are great, and they bear their circumstances with resignation.

The Lord, however, did not want mankind to remain in perpetual stagnation. Therefore did He provide leaven for that dough. He created certain spirits who differ from the mass in that their souls are stirred by dreams. They can see a better world than the one in which they are set.

Their dream will not permit them to stay in the swamp. It burns in them like a fire, sending them towards greener pastures. But they are not content to go alone. They are the leaven whose agitation causes the entire inert mass of humanity to rise along with them.

There are those who cannot envisage castles when they are only dreams. And they prefer a swamp in the hand to a castle in the air. Such men frequently lead the abuse which is often the lot of the world's dreamers. The dreamer is denounced for subverting the social order, for being a trouble maker, but he only meant to detach us from something which has ceased to be good, to something better which is beckoning on the horizon. The dreamer troubles us only because he wants to help us.

Children will on occasions scratch the hand of the doctor who has come to heal them. And the world has often been similarly ungracious to its benefactors, those who have dreamt its noblest dreams. But true healers do their work, undaunted by such folly.

The Human Problem

John's mistake may be traced back to an advertisement. He once saw a picture of perfect relaxation; it was of a man on a fishing boat, his face tanned, and eager for the catch, his sleeves rolled up. The caption said that this man had mastered the wisdom of living. He had bought annuities when he was young, which enabled him, now that he had retired, to spend his days in relaxation and fun.

John determined to do likewise. He liquidated his business and put his money into securities. His income was more than ample for all his needs. Now he was determined to really enjoy life. His imagination danced with all kinds of exciting adventures to which he would give himself.

His first few months were fun: he took a cruise, he did a lot of fishing, he played golf, he went to the races and enjoyed a few card games, but before long he began to feel bored, for his life became too placid, too tranquil. What had been fun at the end of a busy day's work had become meaningless when it only followed upon...more holiday. A life of continual relaxation was unbearably monotonous, and John soon knew that he had made a tragic blunder.

Retirement has been a false ideal in modern life. Some have chosen it voluntarily, while it has been enforced upon others. Aged people have been rejected from industry, and denied the opportunity of productive life. Pensions cannot compensate for the lack of opportunity to be creative.

Man was born to be an active participant in the enterprise of life. His job is to build, serve, create; to satisfy some human need, to add a little to the world's perfection. Any human being who fails to perform this role will be obsessed with the dullness of life, since all his creative energies lie dormant and are pressing for release. When they are not released, he is miserable.

The human condition – man's fate – is not governed solely by economics. Those who have dealt with man's problems only within a financial framework, have oversimplified the human situation. The possession of an ample income cannot sustain a man's life.

Every man was meant to be a builder of the world, and it is only when his body and spirit are bent to the task of building that he can be happy.

Frontiers

Life is an adventure because we are always faced with a frontier. There is always a beyond to lure us on. Our attainments never unravel the total mystery of existence; they can never make the world wholly our own. The line of our attainment merely shifts the frontier forward, and defines the next task against which we must pit our strength.

There are some people who have been so impressed with the trophies won in one campaign that they are content to sit back in self-admiration. They then fall prey to the illusion of self-sufficiency. They feel complete, satisfied. And even when the opportunities for new experiences come their way, they do not see them, for their eyes are fixed on their own backyard, and they cannot discern what beckons from the far horizon.

The adventurous life cannot be sustained on the material level alone. It must be augmented by the spiritual. For while there is a limit to what we can use of material things, there is no limit to what we can enjoy in the way of beauty and truth, in the pursuits of mercy and loving-kindness. Those who seek to continue the quest for material possessions, as the sole means of experiencing life's adventure, will become the enemies of society. Those who turn their attention to spiritual things become the benefactors of the human race.

It is a great tragedy that many people, after attaining a certain measure of material possession, become aware of the futility of further striving in that direction, yet do not transfer their efforts to another level. A great boredom sets into their lives. They feel stagnant, empty, without the zest to carry on with the routine of their existence. Life can be exciting but only at the frontier, where we feel the irresistible call of new goals.

Happy is the man who lives with the knowledge of his own inadequacy. In meeting the challenge of that inadequacy, he finds the deepest meaning of his existence.

True Friendship

One of my dearest friends walked off offended with me yesterday. He misjudged something I had said, and he felt that I had insulted his dignity. I hope I have corrected his impression, but the incident has left me with a troubled feeling.

Are not all human words possible of misjudgment? And is not every human relationship therefore vulnerable? I had become aware of the fact that I had been misjudged and so I was able to explain myself. How often do these misjudgments go unnoticed, producing rifts that widen? Many a friendship has died across a chasm created by an unfortunate word, a word innocently spoken but unfortunately misunderstood.

There is only one solution to avoid such misjudgments. The love we cherish for our friends must be deeper and surer. A love that is deeper and surer will automatically furnish a more sympathetic point of view towards our friends, and its warmth will melt the frigidity which is the outcome of misunderstanding.

The Art of Scrubbing

The disciple said to the master: 'You continually assert the need for repentance. Yet we are not a company of sinners; we are your trusted disciples who have endeavored to follow your example in our lives. Can you teach us the true meaning of repentance, as you see it pertaining to our lives?'

The master replied: 'Go, my son, to the creek on the outskirts of the town. Watch for a week what transpires there. Meditate on it. Then report to me. After you have done this you will understand the meaning of repentance.'

The disciple carried out the instructions of the master. He finally returned, still baffled by his old question, and baffled even more by the strange procedure his master had suggested to him. 'All I saw were women doing their laundry by the creek,' he reported. 'They came with dirty garments, scrubbed them clean, and at the end of the week they returned with more dirty garments to scrub them clean all over again.'

'My son,' said the master, 'this is all you need to learn about repentance. Our souls are like those garments scrubbed by the women. In our encounter with the world, our souls become soiled, and they must be scrubbed repeatedly. Repentance is a kind of scrubbing, to remove the filth which is on our souls. And cleansing must be continuous because the assault of filth is continuous.'

And the master continued: 'All of us must struggle against that filth. Indeed, you and I must struggle even more zealously than most, since a coarse garment does not show its stains as readily as a silken garment. No one can live in the world without being soiled by it. A saint is not one whose soul is unstained, but rather one who has mastered the art of frequent scrubbing.'

The Soap and Water of Life

'But I washed my face yesterday,' Johnny protested. His protests were in vain. His mother insisted that he must wash again, and Johnny was on the road to learning one of life's precious truths, that cleanliness is not a goal to be attained in one bold stroke of achievement, but a goal which must be constantly sought.

Have you ever considered that this is also the key to moral cleanliness? Goodness is not something that can ever be attained with dramatic finality, but it must be fought for and won again every day of our lives.

The filth that attaches to us is not only physical; it is also moral. The fortitude with which we met yesterday's crises has worn thin when the day was done, and courage needs renewal. The dykes of our homes were attacked by a momentary display of temper yesterday, and the same - or a similar – storm may break against them another day. Will the dykes hold? Many a man has steered a honorable course in business until the one great temptation which promised so much and which he could not resist.

A once clean face must be cleansed again when the day is done. The dykes need constant repair against the ravages of the elements. And good character has to be maintained with unending vigilance.

That is why Judaism demands continual self-examination as the key to a sound moral life. The encounter with the world begets stains in our character, stains which can be cleaned only by the soap and water of continued repentance.

Independence

One of man's most common dreams is to achieve independence. Yet it is in some respects a foolish dream. A man cannot live in a vacuum. And living in the society of other people means that we take from them, and give to them in return. What we take or what we give may differ, but giving and taking is of the very essence of life.

It is not only those with obvious needs who are dependent on another's bounty. The parent gives to the child his boundless love, but the child gives as much in return. For the opportunity to love is a precious gift, without which we should be miserable.

We are much too often aware of what we give; we don't always consider what we receive. We extend a helping hand to a neighbor, we feed the fish or the birds, we tend our garden with loving care, we lavish something of ourself upon someone else. But our happiness depends, among other things, on that act of giving. Those we help may depend on us, but in another sense we are dependent on them for the functioning of a vital part of our lives: the need to give.

The man who has music in his soul can quicken a song-starved world. But he cannot fulfill himself by singing to his own soul alone. He is dependent on the world to hear his song and to share in his inspiration.

Woe unto those who try to live independently, who cut the threads linking them to the rest of the world. They have doomed themselves to frustration. Truly we need each other. We need to give, as we need to receive.

Man and the Machine

Is man a machine? The comparison between a man and a machine has occasionally been made. But it is an absurd comparison, and it reveals the ultimate failure in man's understanding of himself.

Man operates by a coordination of many delicate and highly differentiated parts, as does a machine. But a machine did not devise itself. Man, on the other hand, plays a decisive role in his own growth, and he steers himself continually towards the mastery of the powers by which he functions. The machine is static, while man has the power to grow and change.

The machine needs a person to manipulate it, it responds to a directing intelligence. In man the directing intelligence resides in his own being.

Man is a directing intelligence within a miraculously wrought instrument – the body – which performs its work in the world.

Man's Essential Nobility

Some of the gravest incidents of human cruelty also yield evidence of man's essential nobility.

Why have aggressors accompanied their deeds of cruelty with a campaign of abuse against their victims if not to persuade themselves that what they were fighting was really evil, and its destruction was therefore a boon to humanity.

There are some sick minds that appear to get a fiendish satisfaction in hurting and destroying. Sometimes they will seek to hurt and destroy themselves. Sometimes their fury is directed outwards – towards their fellow humans. But the actions of diseased minds offer no clue to the essential character of the normal man, any more than the strange convulsions of a patient racked with fever offer a clue to the nature of the healthy physique.

The aggression of the Nazis, for example, was always preceded by a propaganda offensive. The big lie had to do its work – to present the victim as despicable. Only then could the German people be drawn to perform atrocities. These atrocities, in the emotional climate in which they occurred, seemed to their perpetrators as noble and heroic acts against the enemies of humanity. The sick minds of the Nazi leadership stewed an unholy brew, and unwittingly many innocent men drank from it and were poisoned. With the poison in them, they acted as beasts.

But the fact that they had to be fed poison before their humanity was repressed emphasizes that, left to himself, man is a noble being, capable of justice, mercy, and love.

On the Installment Plan

We speak in installments, as no one is able to speak his mind in full. A single idea is born in our mind, but we cannot communicate it all at once, so we begin a process of elaboration. Words, phrases, sentences are created to introduce our idea, to justify it, to illustrate it, to surround it with the proper qualifications which will establish its truth.

Our elaborations are not always complete, and this is one of the reasons that misunderstandings are widespread. Our ideas are challenged and then we offer further justification. But what happens when we are not present to offer that added clarification of our thought? Then the misunderstanding is deepened, unless someone else is willing to speak on our behalf.

Every utterance, whether ancient or contemporary, is like a text which requires, for its proper understanding, a running commentary, and furthermore, the commentary itself occasionally needs further interpretation. Life may be short, but arguments are endless.

If you should take exception to some idea, do not rush to reject it. The originator may not have expressed himself fully. His speech is deficient – it lacks a clarifying installment. If this be offered, hear it sympathetically. And if no other interpreter be present, try to clarify it yourself.

No concept developed by the human mind is a total falsehood. It may offer a partial truth, but a partial truth is not a lie. You can, if you are brave and resourceful enough, supply the missing part. And then you will have a fuller truth.

Underbrush

The Ammonoosuc River flows behind the house where we spend our summers, in the outskirts of Bethlehem, N.H. But I was never able to see it in all its natural beauty till the day we cleared the underbrush which had grown up on its bank.

I have had a similar sensation with people. Men and women who seemed to me crude and vulgar, devoid of finer sensibilities, have on occasions revealed a nobler self which I never suspected. Circumstances had built up in them negative attitudes which were a kind of underbrush on the bank of their lives, keeping from view the real self, with its inherent glory.

The realization that the people we look at are often hidden by a covering underbrush argues for a wider human understanding. The woman who is so cynical and harsh in your contacts with her is often, beneath the surface, a tenderhearted soul. She has been hurt. She is afraid to love the world again, because her love has been spurned and she recoils from another encounter, which she fears will only yield her more frustration.

The man who argues that the dollar is one's best friend, and that spiritual pursuits are an illusion may really be appeasing his conscience, which keeps on challenging the goals on which he has chosen to stake his own life. A smile is not necessarily a clue to a kindly heart, and a frown does not necessarily reveal a harsh spirit.

Those who really want to understand life must forever keep clearing away the underbrush. Don't judge a person by his expression, which may be a deceiving mask. Reach more deeply into his being, to see the face behind the mask, to see the spirit without distortion. When the underbrush is cleared, you will behold the wonder of a newly revealed glory.

Hurt Souls

When a beast is discontented, it turns vicious. And thus it is with man.

There are occasions when we encounter people who seem vicious. They are aggressive and mean. They magnify petty grievances and are easily provoked to anger. By nature they appear to demand some continual object on which to direct their indignation and abuse. They will not hesitate to strike their fellow man, under the slightest pretext, either with blows or with words. But this expression of viciousness is only incidental. Every vicious act begins inwardly, in a troubled and discontented soul.

When one encounters a vicious act there may not be time for therapy. The immediate response may have to be only in kind, but we shall never get peace by trading blows. Viciousness in action is only a reminder that a hurt soul is waiting to be healed.

Hurt souls are difficult to heal, and they cannot be cured by merely satisfying external wants, for the deep discontent that explodes into viciousness is engendered ultimately not by unfulfilled wants, but by a failure to accept ourselves, despite our limitations. The failure to accept our destinies is at the root of an unsatiable unrest that drives us to distraction. The person who is in revolt against himself cannot be at peace with his fellow man. Seen in relation to eternity, every man's destiny is God's will for him. We and the world will never know peace until we condition ourselves to accept God's will.

Only as a man fulfills the commandment to love himself is he emotionally free to love his fellow man.

The Debt to Our Parents

Joan and Henry were engaged to be married. The preparations were many and harassing, but they had strong nerves, and they managed to attend to everything without becoming short tempered. But a profound disagreement finally developed over the invitations.

Henry had quarrelled with his parents, and he was not living at home. He felt bitter towards them, and did not see why he should invite them. 'They were always mean to me,' he said. 'I owe them nothing.'

Joan knew of Henry's state of mind, and she felt that this was the time to let bygones be bygones, to put an end to the silly feud. She insisted on inviting them.

The argument continued and as Henry berated his parents, Joan became sympathetic towards them. She felt an intense eagerness to meet them, to learn more about them. Had she not quarrelled more than once with her own parents? Yet she knew how much they meant to her. And she felt it her mission to mediate between Henry and his father and mother.

Joan asked Henry for a picture of his parents, and he produced one. Joan looked at it intently, and then she was struck by a strong resemblance. Henry had his mother's eyes, and his father's broad smile. She liked the look of both of them.

'See,' she exclaimed. 'It was your mother and father who first introduced you to me. The first things I noticed which made you stand out from the crowd at the dance when we met were your eyes and your smile. Without those, you would not be you, and I could not love you as much as I do.'

Henry was not prepared for this turn of the argument. But he did not yield easily. Then Joan thought of the final move. 'Perhaps you owe them nothing,' she said, 'but I owe them very much. I'll include them in the list of my guests. No,' she added on further reflection, 'they are my special friends, and we'll visit them together before we are married.'

It took Henry some time to overcome his pride but finally he had to yield to his bride's greater wisdom. It was a slow but also a sure awareness that impressed itself upon him, and then he knew not only with his mind but with his heart that his parents must be at his wedding, because they had shared in making that day of happiness possible for him.

GOD'S PRAYER

Every day
When prayers rise
In synagogue, church and mosque,
God prays for His world.
May it be the will of My children
To accept My gift of life,
And allow Me to lead them
Toward the light.

Free Love

True love is always free.
I did not merit
That God call me
From the infinite void
To give me life
And adorn me
With His image,
Enabling me
To think and dream,
To feel and serve.
I did not merit
The love of those who raised me
To the time of my blooming.
All lavished love on me
Beyond my deserving.

When I rise
To a higher love
I, too, shall bestow it free.
Love is the soul's answer to God,
Calling me to be like Him.
The gift of love nourishes the world.

Love is a Kind of Bondage

If you know a man who loves his family or his God, then pity him. For love is a kind of bondage, and he who has yielded to love has forfeited his peace.

The indifferent can walk the world undisturbed. But he who has given his heart in love is vulnerable to a thousand hurts. Every mishap that befalls the one he loves brings him grief. A child's illness, a wife's indisposition, a friend's sorrow, the perils which face his country—each of them distills disquiet in his soul. If he loves God then he has extended even wider the zone of his concern. He is forever troubled by a yearning to serve God and make his life acceptable in God's sight. Love is a hard task-master.

The word care holds a double connotation: affection as well as anxiety. The two are indeed related. Let a person but care for someone or something and he will become subject to many cares concerning them.

Only by shrinking the zone of love can we reduce our exposure to life's hazards. He who sheds the love for parents, or wife, or children, or friends, frees himself from anxieties because of what happens to them. And total freedom is enjoyed only by those who have never been born. Whoever wants life must accept the commitment to love and all the cares that go with it. Life is a continuous response to disturbance, while he who is wholly carefree, wholly indifferent and unconcerned, might as well be dead.

With Uncertain Steps

A light shines, but it illumines only part of the way, and I must walk my course with uncertain steps.

My religious tradition, the mores and customs of society, the law of the land—all these tell me what is right and what direction I must follow. And an inner light— my conscience—prods me to make one choice or another. But all this is only a partial light and it does not clearly indicate the path that I am to take.

I am told to be generous, and to spend some of my energy and my substance in service to others. But how much of my energy and my substance must I spend to meet the commitment of generosity? And who are the others I am to serve? I cannot serve all and I must make a selection, but by what criteria do I select some and ignore others? I am told to obey the law of the land, but my country may be pursuing policies which deeply offend my conscience. Shall I support the actions of my country though it brings me anguish? Shall I be silent and bear my distress quietly? Or shall I become an activist in resisting what I believe to be wrong?

Every choice I make is based on certain facts and circumstances I consider relevant. But the facts I know only partially, and my weighing of their significance is pathetically fallible and often short-sighted. This is why I must be ready continually to review and reassess my decision in the light of added knowledge and wisdom which the years will hopefully bring me.

Like a Fountain

There are riches of all kinds. Some are acquired by saving, while others grow not by saving, but by spending.

My ability to love is enhanced as I draw on it and expend it in acts of love. If I should hoard it and leave it unused it will dwindle and I will become impoverished; I will become increasingly withdrawn and self-centered.

A mind that is not activated, that is not drawn on to read and think, will gradually grow sluggish. Like the body that is not exercised, its energies will wither away, and I will become the poorer for it.

As I spend myself on the world around me, I become a richer and more vital self. But if I spare myself, I diminish myself.

Like the fountain which becomes more abundant as it is drawn on, so is man, in some important areas of his life. The more we save, the less we have, and the more we spend, the more we have.

Life's Larger Drama

The caterpillar must die so that the butterfly might emerge from it.

On the human scene this process works more subtly, but it is discernible there. We live as long as we are needed to care for the young, and to raise them until they are launched to be on their own. Then we begin to decline and in due time, once our work is done, we reach our twilight and finally withdraw.

A generation goes and a generation comes; it is only because a generation goes that another generation can come, to enact its own odyssey of existence, and then to enact its own cycle of growth, maturing and decline.

Each stage in the death-life cycle elicits its own emotions from us, but it is good to see the vicissitudes of existence from the perspective of the larger drama at play in the universe.

Man's True Freedom

A deed is virtuous when it is performed in freedom. When our hand is forced to act by external pressures, then our action ceases to be either good or evil. Morality rests in the inner disposition, in the free association of the will with the actions we perform.

God does not paralyze the hand that is raised to perform an evil act. He does not silence the lips that are about to utter a falsehood. The sun shines on the good and the evil alike. The rain fructifies the earth of all who till it, regardless of the moral quality of their lives.

The internal forces God implanted in man to aid his work will likewise perform their accustomed service, never discriminating between one person or another. The imagination, the power to endure, the quality of courage, the satisfaction in carrying through difficult undertakings

—these will play their accustomed role in the man struggling to advance righteousness, and also in the man struggling to promote some evil scheme that will imperil the world. In short, God helps every man to become what he wants to be.

We become what we want to be, but we do not necessarily remain what we have become. For only the way of virtue is the enduring way, while the evil way is a dead end road from which we are meant to return. The fruit of evil is bitter, and we soon discover it. And after we have had a chance to travel some distance on an evil way, God asserts Himself to call us back to Himself. He stirs the conscience to renewed action. He disturbs us with an inner unrest; He strikes us with a sense of guilt. Persistently, He whispers to us: "You have had your way and you have made a fool of yourself; now come back to Me." This is the source of repentance by which a gracious God enables us to correct ourselves, to renounce the evil and return to the good.

A Wider Love

Moralists have sometimes asked the impossible. They have asked that we become selfless, that we ignore the call of our own personal interests and become zealous lovers of the rest of mankind.

This is not only impossible; it is also a perverted ideal. Why should we love the rest of mankind? Is it because people are sacred, because they are God's highest creation, and we please God by loving those whom He loves? But if people are sacred, are we not sacred also? And if we are summoned to love other people, should not our love begin at home?

The failure to treat people with loving consideration has been a source of tragedy in the world. But the tragedy is no less grave when love is withdrawn from one's own self. A wholesome person must care deeply about himself; he must attend to his bodily needs; he must seek fulfillment of the deepest impulse residing in his heart. Otherwise, he will be frustrated and miserable.

The frustrated person has injured not only himself; he has injured God's plan for creation. For to each person God has imparted a special measure of excellence with which to enrich all life. The frustrated person cannot serve; his excellence is inhibited; he is but a part of himself. We can love God and man only when we express ourselves with all our heart, with all our soul and all our might.

All good things are good within a measure. Love should begin at home, but it must not end there. A selfish person is one who can love only himself, his self is the boundary where his love halts. But one can err also by being completely selfless, by allowing his own self to be submerged by the pressures of life, by disregarding the claims and possibilities of his own nature. A moral man has mastered a wider love. He loves the world without surrendering his love for himself.

God Shrank His Providence

The sun that gives warmth can sometimes be too lavish, and scorch and burn. Love is the same way; it is good, but not in excess.

The Gifts of Life and Love

A parent who permits his love for his child to flow without limit will thwart his growth. A wise parent must shrink his love, to permit the child an area where he stands alone, unprotected, to test his own strength as a growing person. The child must be permitted to walk from here to there, though he might stumble and suffer mishap.

God's way with the world follows the same procedure. Theoretically He could have made His providence coextensive with the total life of all His creatures. He could have planned the world so as to have perfection reign everywhere. We would have been spared much trouble in such a world, but we would have been denied one very precious blessing—the privilege to stand on our own feet, to grow through our own effort, to know the thrill of discovery, of vanquishing evil and advancing the good.

God, therefore, shrank his providence, releasing a realm of life to be the theatre for our own free development. The disorder in our world—the world within and the world without—is the area God excluded from His own providence, to give man a noble task, the task of growing in perfection through the exercise of his freedom.

Before Darkness Falls

Our appreciation of life is enhanced when we find it imperiled. When we confront forces that would destroy life and obliterate it, then we experience a new surge of love for it, and a new desire to cherish it and preserve it.

The problem of man is that he waits for a time when life is imperiled to respond with these wonderful attributes. When life moves in a normal groove and no

157

crisis threatens, we are content to remain insensitive. We remain insensitive to what we do to ourselves, and we remain insensitive to what we do or fail to do to others. The American people will smoke 551 billion cigarettes this year, 11 billion more than last year, even though medical science has repeatedly warned us that there is a correlation between smoking and lung cancer. What would not a person struck with the disease do to hold on to life? But sometimes the awakening comes too late. I know of a man who was blessed with good health, a good family, a good business, but he socialized with the wrong crowd and he eventually was drawn to gambling. In the end it ruined him. Looking over the wreckage of his own life, he has often said: "What wouldn't I do if I could start over again?" Sometimes we can start over again, but sometimes our wisdom comes too late.

Must we wait for the moment of impending doom to retrace our steps when we know the course we have embarked on is the wrong course? It is dangerous to wait for the moment of final return—for we may miscalculate and reach the moment of no return. A wise man cherishes life and the things that make life livable without waiting for the face of disaster to show itself.

Awe and Mystery

The more we discover the nature of our world and of ourselves, the more we are stirred to feel a sense of awe. The wisdom disclosed to our probing minds is so wondrous that we cannot find words potent enough duly to describe it. And the wisdom is disclosed to us wherever we turn.

Perhaps the greatest marvel that should move us to awe is the phenomenon of individuality. No two creatures have the same appearance, the same voice, or the same bent of mind. Every finger registers a different print, each person's ear is something special and unique, each flake of snow reveals a different design under the microscope. A scientist announced recently that his study of the habits of penguins showed that these creatures will return to their nests from distances of many thousands of miles, that penguins recognize their mates by their voices after many months of separation, and that once mated they remain faithful to their mates throughout life.

It is this sense of awe at the divine mystery which makes us truly human. All other needs we share with creatures below us—the need for food, clothes, shelter, a mate. But only man can rise to consciousness of himself and his world and react to the mystery disclosed as a mystery. For only he knows the grandeur of thought and its limitation, and only he can therefore be stirred to awe, as he encounters the magnificence that surpasses the human.

The Self We are and the Self We want to Be

Thought is potent, but not nearly as potent as we would sometimes like to believe. There are many forces which impinge on us, and they push us in one direction or another, often in clear defiance of our better judgment.

We all have more wisdom than we put to use in the normal round of our existence. Many a man knows that he ought not to smoke, but he smokes; that he ought not to gamble, but he gambles; that he ought to be patient and forgiving, but he is impatient and vindictive. If we only lived by what we knew! But we know with the mind, and our life is only partially under the mind's control.

The growth of character is a slow achievement. It is born of struggle, the struggle against habit, against emotional inclination. Wisdom makes us aware of the need to struggle against these forces which keep us in bondage to our lower self. It takes, however, an act of will to engage in this struggle, and the willingness to bear the pain of resistance, the resistance of the self we are, to the self we want to become.

Shall We Always Forgive?

The ready forgiveness of a malicious and knowing evil would only encourage the further commission of evil, and prove a disservice to society. It would also be a disservice to the evil-doer for it would fail to challenge him to change his ways. Such forgiveness is an abdication of the duty to pursue justice and curb deeds of evil.

Does this mean that once an evil deed has been committed it dooms its doer forever after, and there is no way for him to extricate himself from it? Not at all! A man can try to atone for his wrongdoing. There is available what we call in Hebrew "teshuvah" or penitence, as expressed in remorse and the attempt at restitution.

It would, of course, have been difficult for Eichmann to repent. For him to acknowledge the full gravity of his own evil, he would have had to loathe himself with a degree of loathing beyond normal human endurance. This is perhaps one reason why he did not repent—he had gone too far now to turn back.

God is a loving and forgiving Father; and man, when he rises to divine heights, practices forgiveness as well. But he who is to be forgiven must merit these graces. He may merit them by changing the way of his life.

Principles Are Not Enough

Thought is our abiding necessity. We may adopt great principles which seemingly cover every one of life's predicaments, but principles do not automatically apply themselves and we need an ongoing effort of reason to decide the measure of relevance in our principles to the specific issues which challenge us.

We say that we must love our children and we also say that we must discipline them. But when shall we show softness and when shall we show sternness? When does love spoil the child and when does discipline become unrelenting and excessively severe? We believe that good government imposes a minimum of interference on the citizen, but what is that minimum? We say that peace is indispensable to survival, but we also say that at some point the nation's interests may have to be defended, even at the cost of war. But where is that point? When shall we compromise for the sake of peace, and when shall we stand unyielding for our "rights"?

Without a body of principles to guide us, we would be altogether lost amidst conflicting alternatives which bid for our attention. But having a body of principles does not relieve us of the need to grapple with the problem of what to believe and how to act.

The Dream is Real

Some people like to call themselves realists, and they look with disdain upon the dreamers. But only the dream is real, only the dream can energize life and sustain it in the face of hardship.

A person who has deep feelings as to what he would like to make of himself will be fired by zeal to strive. A nation fired by some great purpose will be dynamic and resourceful. The dream may be good or bad. Hitler's dream set the world aflame but it mobilized all the latent energies of the German people and set them to assume formidable tasks.

Every forward movement in civilization had its first beginnings in a dream. And the unfinished business of civilization, to build a world of peace among all men and all nations, will likewise fall into the same pattern. The deeds by which this goal will find its fulfillment will be motivated and energized by the dream, by the hope.

The dream, when it is cherished long enough, seriously enough, will be evocative of the strength to carry it to realization. The dream thus carries a double efficacy. It helps give direction to the shape of the real world, and, at the same time, it endows life with purpose and vitality.

THE SECRET OF MYSELF

I came from the infinite void
In the miracle of life's renewal.
I bore with me
The secret of myself,
Known by none other,
He gave me
A boundary of time,
A part of His garden to tend,
And skills enough to work.
But no more,

That I be not distracted
By other claims.

Like clay in the potter's hand
He formed me to be what I am,
Small and frail,
Yet noble,
To be His partner
In the work of creation.

Of Time and Life

Time is the duration of life and life is God's creation. And part of what God created when He created life is a span of time for each creature to be born, to grow, to attain its maturing, to decline and to pass away from the scene of its labors. By the way we live, by the play of circumstances, we may fall short of the time allotted to us, or we may hold on to the time of our life and live it to its maximum possibility. But there is an end to every life under the sun, and rich man or poor man, the great and the humble alike are subject to the same law. They must all live within a boundary, a boundary of time, and when they near the edge of the boundary they must be ready to bow out from the scene.

We grieve when someone dear to us has reached the boundary, and it is right that we grieve. But our grief is mitigated by the knowledge that every day of life is the renewal of a miracle, the miracle of life, and if those we have lost are precious to us, then we must be grateful for whatever time they were permitted to be at our side. Nor must we be upset when we ourselves come to the boundary. There is just so much in the cup of wine. Drink what you are given and be glad that you were privileged to taste of the wine of life. And when you have reached the end, graciously pass the cup to other hands waiting to receive it.

Hurrying Life

Time is our servant, we must never permit it to become our master. The train leaves at 3:59, the plane departs at 7:58, the curtain goes up at 7:45, the whistle will blow at 12:01. If we don't watch out we become the slaves of a schedule. Since time is duration of experience we are occasionally tempted to hurry time, thinking we will enhance our experiences. But when we hurry time we shrink life. For the faster we go, the less we see. The Swiss Alps are awesome in their grandeur, but when we fly over them by jet we hardly notice them. A melody must be sung to a certain cadence. If we speed it, we destroy its beauty.

We must allow time for the sake of living. We must allow time to read and think; we must allow time for friends if we want to have friends; we must allow time for worship if we are to cultivate any meaningful religious life; we must allow time for our family—to cultivate the togetherness of shared experience and even to be able to settle an occasional argument. Hurrying life may enable us to have more experiences but the experiences will be shallow and unsatisfying. It is better to go slower, to have fewer experiences, but to live in depth and to enjoy each event to its maximum possibility.

A New Page

Time has continuity but it also has its own identity. What we do one day conditions what we can do the next day. But each unit of time, each year, each day that breaks on the horizon has its own identity, its own being, and it need not be lived in the shadow of yesterday. If we so will it we can turn a new day in a new direction, to correct old blunders, and to reach out to embrace new possibilities. It is in this freedom of time that man is offered the greatest opportunity for self-fulfillment. Yesterday we allowed foolish thoughts or unworthy passions to sway us. Yesterday men faced one another as enemies thrusting hostile words at one another. Yesterday, in some part of the world, men fired deadly weapons at one another and snuffed out life, precious life, tender and youthful life, destroying what God had given. But today and all the todays which will follow it can be turned in a new direction, to live with wisdom, to help realize the unity of the human family under the common fatherhood of God. Whoever broods on yesterday and its mistakes and its heartaches is hugging something which is no more, and he is spurning something freshly born which beckons him.

Today begins a new page in the volume of eternity. Dip your pen in ink and write, and let it be a noble composition, to testify that you know the value of time.

Life is Fragile

God made life fragile, sensitive, and vulnerable to all

kinds of hurts. We cannot fathom the mind of God, but whoever has probed life deeply has come to recognize that all of life's experiences, if properly used, can deposit a plus rather than a minus on the scale of our existence. And there are certain gains for man which he can come upon only through being hurt, through knowing pain, through bearing upon himself the evidence of life's fragile quality.

We can understand and feel with others only to the extent that we have been in their place. The successful man, in business or a profession, will think smugly that the one who has fallen behind is a "shlemiel." The successful man would profit by an occasional failure, it would teach him a lesson in humility.

Life is precious, and life needs to be preserved. There is a need to be compassionate and tender, to cultivate a quality of mercy to match our strength. It is the occasional breakdown of health, the occasional experience of pain, the occasional frustration of our plans and purposes, that sharpens our sensitivity and makes us feel with others, that allows us to see ourselves in their place and to know the problems with which they grapple. Only as we learn to feel with others, do we become truly human.

No one is invited to choose suffering deliberately, but when it comes, it is well to embrace it as another opportunity to see life in larger dimensions.

A Standard by Which to Judge

Only those who know truth can recognize falsehood.

The Hebrew prophets bore in their hearts a vision of the ideal and when their world contradicted that ideal, they knew that their world was wrong and they rejected it. This is the value of our religious heritage—it gives us a standard by which to judge the world around us. Our path may sometimes take us among people who are dishonest, who cheat on their fellow-man, who are unfaithful to their families, who are false to their God, who are disloyal to their country. Without a vision of what is right we are always in danger of accepting the world we encounter as normal and do as others do. Those who have a standard can be discriminating.

The person who knows harmony will recognize disharmony and recoil from it. One who knows the meaning of justice will have no trouble in recognizing—and rejecting—injustice. The possession of a moral standard is like the possession of a compass while sailing on the open sea—it will help prevent our going off course.

The New in the Old

A person represents a point in the line of the universal movement of existence. He cannot detach himself from that line to become other than what he is. Our physical and our human environment, after some time, become more or less fixed; our own biological constitution, born of the stuff of heredity and the fresh endowment of the Creator, is a constant which cannot be replaced.

Our world is old but it need not be monotonous, for the new and the old are not contradictory; there is a dimension of newness in the old. He who looks at the world with a perceiving eye will behold continually aspects of newness in the old and the familiar. The song we heard a hundred times has qualities of freshness each time we listen to it. The picture we love never grows overly familiar; qualities of fresh interest reveal themselves each time we gaze at it. A poem is never old. We may read it times without end and each reading will register nuances of insight we have not encountered before. The people we love never bore us. They release a new radiance, a new warmth, and a new joy each time we are with them.

The world is old, certainly, and this is our home. The trees, the mountains, the stars, the teeming creatures who inhabit the earth with us—they have all been here before we arrived on the scene. Foolish are the people who think they can satisfy the longing for newness by changing the external setting of their lives. What we need to change is our outlook. Blessed is the perceiving eye for it will bring great meaning into our lives. It will enable us to see the new in the old.

Fear

Many people are buying tranquilizers from all kinds of quack doctors who are doing a fabulous business in our society, whereas what they need is just a good dose of old-fashioned fear.

There are people destroying their health, eating what they should not eat, smoking when they should not smoke, gambling when they should not gamble, quarreling when they should not quarrel, rushing when they should be still.

They do these things though they have been warned that this is a perilous road to travel on. They have hardened their heart not to listen, not to heed, not to be afraid.

Fear of the consequences would save them, but complacency will be their undoing.

There are people who are undermining their family life by doing and saying foolish things, proceeding in the smug assumption that it does not matter. You cannot raise good children unless you are a little afraid as you proceed about the consequences of certain developments. Fear is the mother of vigilance. Smugness, complacency, hardness of heart—these are the marks of recklessness, and recklessness is the open door to disaster.

Our world is surrounded by divine powers ready to support every good endeavor. But just as man cannot do God's part, God will not do man's part. And man must work strenuously to face the perils which beset his life. Complacency, hardness of heart, is the road to misfortune, while the happy man is the one who knows when to exercise the virtue of being afraid.

ONLY A SOUL

A face is a mask
Worn by a soul.
The soul dreams, hopes, suffers,
But only faint traces
Show on the mask.
The eye sees the mask,
Only a soul can see a soul
Groping to find its way
To God.

To Be Fully Human

An object reveals its significance not in the elements which it has in common with all other objects, but in the qualities which set it apart and give it individuality.

A person is part of the hierarchy of life. He is sprung by a long line of evolution from simpler creatures, whose counterparts still live in the kingdom of the beasts. But we shall never know man if we see him only in terms of the elements he shares with beasts. Man is truly human when he is seen in terms of the qualities which are his own, which set him apart from the rest of creation.

A man must respect his total self, which includes the elements that link him with the animal. But he remains an animal unless he also lives on the human plane, unless he cultivates the elements that constitute his human individuality.

The pleasurable sensations of eating and drinking and mating are available also to the animal. When life is centered on the quest for the pleasure of the palate, or of sex, we are living on the subhuman level. What makes us human is that we can think or dream, that we can follow the call to justice and feel stirred by the passion for truth, that we can sacrifice self-interest for the sake of higher ideals. The highest mark of our humanity is that we can think of God and love Him and serve Him. It is to the extent that we cultivate our distinctive attributes as persons that we become fully human.

A Partnership

Man's world moves on its course through the collaboration of two directing influences: God and man. From the hand of the Creator have come the basic drives which stir in each creature and the dimly perceived goals of its life. But directing these drives must be the hand of man who gropes to become conscious of his goals and who must mobilize the resources of his environment and the energies of his own heart and mind in dedicated and purposeful endeavor.

We sometimes lose sight of this partnership. Because God is unseen we sometimes assume that He is absent and we think man is sole master of his world. But we may also err in the opposite direction, forgetting that man has a vital role in the shaping of his destiny. Some religious cults forbid medicine. Desperately ill people have sometimes lost their lives because their religion did not allow surgery or blood transfusion; they depended on God alone to heal them. For centuries people accepted with resignation child mortality, plagues of all kinds, drought, famine and persecution. In whatever transpired they saw God's will and they thought it necessary to submit to it unquestioningly.

Much, very much, comes from the hand of God, but God depends on man to use his own hands in the zone of responsibility that was assigned to human initiative.

The Secret of Our Strength

I once heard a man say: "If I had known in the beginning of life all I would have to go through, I would not have believed it possible that I could make it." In retrospect, as we survey the road by which we have come, we are often appalled by all the difficulties we had to overcome, and we find it difficult to believe that we—the puny *we* we think we are—proved capable of making it.

The truth, of course, is that we *have* made it, that a person's life in retrospect discloses qualities of strength we seldom suspect we could muster but which proved available when we needed them. The man who played Superman in the films—a giant of a man in bodily endowment—proved a weakling in meeting life: he found that his physical prowess was not enough to see him through, and he killed himself. On the other hand, many weaklings proved veritable heroes in doing what often seemed impossible.

Dr. Christian Barnard, whose golden hands pioneered in heart transplant surgery, suffers with arthritis of his hands, and he must take continued medication to keep them mobile. Search the biographies of men who did great things—you find them often to have been people beset with all kinds of weaknesses. Where did Abraham Lincoln get the strength to face domestic discord, the herculean tasks of leading the nation in a time of crisis? Where did he get the strength to endure the abuse heaped on him by North and South? How could he bear the years when the cause of the Union ran consistently at low tide?

Strength is relative. It does not exist in a ready and completed proportion to be invoked when needed. Strength grows, as all other attributes do, when we draw on them. The muscle grows stronger as we use it, our capacity to love grows with every act of loving, and our ability to meet the ordeal of life's problems also grows as we make demands on it. From the infinite reservoir of strength which nourishes the universe we are continually replenished and increased with strength, as we need it. Let a man but throw himself into the work which needs to be done. Strength to pursue it will be given him and he will find he can do what he may at first have thought impossible. God gives strength to the weary, and endows them with vigor to meet life's demands.

You Cannot Measure a Living Tree

Only a fallen tree can be measured for size. A living tree is in a state of growth, and we cannot assess its stature. What it is at the moment is transitory, and it gives way to the tree's continuous unfolding.

And it is so with people. We can say of a man that his life has been distinguished, or otherwise, when his days are ended. Then is the time to render an accounting. But the living are subject to change and they are, therefore, beyond such final judgment.

Is humanity a failure? Is my life but a round of dreams unattained, of goals and purposes unrealized? Is my child in the grip of immature passions which will inhibit him from reaching his hidden possibilities? I have sometimes been overcome by such reflections, but then I remembered that living people are in flux. What they are now is one thing, but tomorrow they may be something else.

We are only at the dawn of man's adventure on earth. Man is not fully man as yet. In the slow evolution of the species, many human qualities now concealed will yet come to light. And my own life and the life of my children is subject to the same law of growth. We are all moving toward a greater maturing of our powers. What we are is an insufficient basis for judging what we can or will be.

Those Who Live on a Mountain

Those who live on a mountain are often unaware of its majesty. We need the perspectives of some distance to see the true dimensions of the world about us.

We are often set amidst great blessings, but we are not sensitive to them. We take our country, with its free institutions, for granted. We may even focus on the fierce problems which beset our country and on the erosions of our liberties which occur in times of crisis and profound civil unrest. The impressive fact, however, is that even in tense and critical times our democratic traditions have survived essentially unscathed, and our basic freedoms have been asserted with uninihibited vigor. Strangers who come to our shores and see us from the outside, with the advantage of the perspective endowed by distance, see a truer sight, and they generally acclaim America as a land truly blessed and as giving its citizens opportunities of self-fulfillment in freedom rarely equalled anywhere else in the world.

In our private world as well, some of us live amidst singular blessings, but take them for granted. We possess good health, a harmonious family life; we have no need to worry about a livelihood. Some of us, nevertheless, go about disgruntled with our lot, depressed in spirit, with deep disquiet written on our faces. It is the old story: he who lives on the mountain does not see its grandeur. We are too close to our own lives and so we lack the perspective to judge. We take our blessings for granted, but concentrate on some problems which persist amidst our blessings.

We must learn to dissociate ourselves from our true condition, to imagine ourselves in the place of other people, in order to gain the perspective to see the truth. It is important to cultivate a perceiving eye which will enable us to see that the mountain is beautiful even when we are privileged to live on top of it.

An Art

This is the most important truth to learn about life, that it is an art.

Some people live life with undisciplined spontaneity. A day dawns and they meet it as it comes, situation by situation. The pressures generated by events direct them along on their course and they respond to those pressures on the basis of impulsive choice. But one cannot create a beautiful painting by merely splashing color on canvas. The splashing of color is the final act of the creative process. In the beginning is thought, in the beginning is a brooding of the spirit. The scene painted is a transformation of a scene encountered in the outer world, transformed to serve the artist as a vehicle for his perception of beauty.

It is not easy to succeed in any art and least of all in the art of living. Success comes to those who know that life is first born in thought, who seek the vision before the deed, and conform the deed to the vision.

Living With Imperfection

There are no supermen on this earth. Human beings are limited, and no one can give us the perfect examplification of what a man ought to be. We must learn to live with imperfection.

What is the art of human relations? It is simply the application of this wisdom: to ignore life's minuses and concentrate on its pluses, to live life and love it, despite the imperfections. No friend will give us perfect understanding every time we turn to him. No teacher will always teach brilliantly or always treat his students with perfect fairness. No parent will always speak softly and calmly. There are no perfect husbands or perfect wives who will always be sweet, reasonable, tolerant and understanding. The world we live in, the people we deal with, have much to offer, but we must live with them despite their failings.

The same art is involved in living with oneself. We cannot demand of ourselves to be always wise, tactful, patient, cheerful. It is human to err, and when we do err, it is wrong to be relentlessly angry with ourselves. We must always strive to improve, but we must begin with the recognition that deficiency is the normal human condition. It is inconsistent with the facts of human nature to reject ourselves for being fallible humans who are often bound to be mistaken.

The fact that we are imperfect gives life its greatest zestfulness. It gives life the glory always to strive for improvement. A man must never settle for what he is, but he must never reject what he is. The road to improvement is endless, but we shall fail miserably unless we realize that here in this imperfect world we are meant to build our home. Here we must find the pluses scattered among the minuses and strive to convert some of the minuses to pluses as a result of our own efforts. We shall never be able to complete this task, but to be engaged in it is glory enough.

Handle With Care

The other day a sanitation truck ran over a squirrel on my street, and passersby watched with visible anguish how this tiny creature struggled for life. We are all compassionate—under some circumstances. Whenever we encounter life in the grip of some destructive force seeking to undo it, we feel aroused. We feel the stirring of an impulse to come to the aid of life, to protect it and to preserve it.

It is when life flows on its normal course and no crisis threatens that we are content to go our way in callous unconcern. The same person who will be terribly upset when someone close to him has been struck with illness will under normal circumstances allow weeks and months to pass without visiting or calling. What would not a person do to save himself when struck with some fatal disease? But how often do we allow ourselves to adopt habits of work and play which are calculated to undermine our health. We care about life—ours and that of others—when we see it visibly and immediately threatened, but under normal circumstances we treat it casually, as though it were a matter of indifference to us.

The truth is that life is always precarious and must always be treated with solicitousness. A wise man loves those close to him—whether by kinship of blood or of sentiment—when he has them, when they are able to enjoy the warmth of his friendship and the tokens of his love. A wise man takes care of his life, his health, his affairs when no crisis threatens his peace.

We have a margin left for mending when things go wrong. We can mend the body with medicine and we can mend the spirit with a spiritual medicine—repentance and inner change. But the time for mending is not without its limit. Some wait too long and they reach a point of no return. Blessed is the man who attains wisdom when he can still make good use of it. All life is fragile; handle it with care.

THE GREENING OF THE WORLD

The fallen leaves,
Lie brown and bent,
Scattered at my feet.
My mind recalls them
In their former pride
As perched in high abode,
They waved and sang
To sun and sky
In life's acclaim.
On rougher days
They bore the heat of sun,

The lashing wind and rain.

The world will green again,
Then green again will turn to brown,
And death will take another toll.
Will they of next spring's birth
Remember those that came and went before
And know they bear
God's constant grace
To green the world
With life's rebirth?

We Die in the Midst of Living

We die in the midst of living. No one ever really brings to completion the goals toward which he has directed his life.

Some goals we reach but then they are at once replaced by new goals which challenge us. Now it is this we want, for ourselves or for our children. But when the *this* has come, we want the *that,* and no sooner has *that* arrived when we want something else. We dream of seeing our child begin school, then we want to see him graduate, then we want to see him in college, then we want to see him marry and become established in some fruitful occupation. And when all these have come to pass do we say, "My goal is now attained"? No, then we dream of seeing a grandchild. No matter what we have attained, there is always a beyond to which we are drawn.

This uncompleted character of life is part of what makes our existence an ongoing adventure. For if we could ever attain a day of feeling that our work is done, what would there remain for us to strive for the day after? A day when there is nothing for us to do is a barren day, a wasted day. Life's satisfaction derives from the struggle, the adventure, rather than from the one final moment of realization. As long as there will be the tasks to challenge us we shall find life aglow with interest.

An Artist Is Never Content

An artist is never content with his work. The truth which inspires his vision is greater than his vision, and his vision is greater than his art.

The moment of his greatest triumph is marred by a touch of sadness. The world may acclaim him as a genius, but he knows his frustrating limitations, how far his work fails to exhaust the richness of life's infinite possibilities. He will never become the perfect artist, but his discontent will help him become a better artist.

The frustration of the artist is only a particular instance of a larger human frustration. Our aspirations fall short of our possibilities, and our achievements fall far short of our aspirations.

We need to find a measure of satisfaction in whatever fulfillments come to us in the course of our quest for a meaningful life. But he who is honest with himself will have his satisfaction marred by the disquieting awareness of his inadequacy. We shall become better people if we are truly aware of our shortcomings.

The Momentum Carries Us Along

Before a runner has started his race, he can turn in one direction or another. But once he has started to run he has generated a momentum and he cannot easily stop or turn back. Life is like that, too. Every action we take releases a momentum that carries us further along on its way, for good or for evil.

After ignoring the sense of guilt accompanying the first transgression, the subsequent transgressions come easier. Adolf Eichmann described his revulsion at the first sight of the blood of his victims. But evil released a momentum and it carried him along, from degradation to degradation, until he had altogether snuffed out the divine spark within him.

Good deeds have the same faculty. They generate a tide and carry the person along with them. Ask any of the heroes of the human race where they gathered the strength to become what they became; the answer will always be the same. They embarked on the journey and then the momentum helped them along.

An ancient sage explained this by saying: "The reward of a good deed is another good deed, and the reward of an evil deed is another evil deed, for every good deed inspires another good deed, and every evil deed inspires another evil deed."

Habit As Servitude

I am what I am, and I do what I do, because of many aids which the Creator has placed at my disposal. One of the most important is my capacity to form habits. I need not burden my mind to think through every question with which I must contend in life. A behavior pattern has set within me, and my responses to many of these questions come automatically.

The time of my retiring at night and rising in the

morning, the style of my work at home and in the office, the casual as well as the serious exchanges with friends and associates, are all governed by a pattern which is largely habituated. Even the letter that I write is only partly original. In fact, it follows a style which has become part of me, and which I draw on whenever I face the need for a written communication. I am not called to confront these questions with fresh originality. The answers come to me readily, almost instinctively; the gift of habit simplifies much of my life.

But habit exacts a price for its benefits. It tends to embrace the future in the arms of the past and inhibits me from fresh confrontations with life. The food I have been accustomed to eat may not be good for me; the companions with whom I have spent my leisure hours may have a bad influence on me. The road on which I walk may be well-trodden, but it may take me to an undesirable destination. At times I need to leave the well-trodden path and blaze a new trail for myself. But all the momentum of my past behavior, all the habituated procedures built up in the course of the years will seek to hold me and inhibit me from making the break.

A pilot flying a plane over long distances will occasionally relent his active control and permit a gadget, a mechanical pilot, to take over. It gives him precious relief from an arduous assignment. But no gadget can take full control; life must never be surrendered to automatic direction by outer mechanisms or inbred habit patterns. The free mind of man must always be ready to resume full control and, when necessary, begin steering in a new direction.

Status Seekers

The status seeker has often been ridiculed in our society. But is not the concern with one's status a legitimate expression of self-respect? It is natural to seek recognition, to gain esteem, to achieve a high sense of personal worth in the eyes of our fellow-men.

Academicians aspire to promotions in rank. The government service, civilian as well as military, rates its members into various categories, and promotions are deeply appreciated and much sought after. Various prizes and honors are awarded to artists and scientists, and these are highly regarded, not so much for their intrinsic worth, as for the status they confer.

The quest for status is not dishonorable, but the manner in which it is sought often is. Too many people pursue status through a false scale of value. Sometimes they will seek to "buy" status by artificially inflating their ego. Publicity agents have been hired to promote the status of their clients by inflating their virtues, sometimes even inventing these virtues. Identifying status with material possessions, men seek to surround themselves with the tokens of wealth: jewels, clothes, furs, cars, houses.

A person rises in status to the extent that he rises in the possession of values which are intrinsic. Outer possessions add little to a man's true worth. Let him grow in character, in qualities of heart and mind, and he will grow correspondingly in the esteem of other men, at least of such men whose esteem is worth enjoying.

We Fashion Our Freedom or Our Bondage

Man, by nature, is free to choose life as he wills. But this freedom is not static. It is continually curtailed or extended, depending on how wisely we plot the course of our existence.

A person who has embarked on a life of crime has, to a great extent, cancelled his freedom to choose the good. He has released pressures which will continue to push him farther on the road of his choice. With every act of dissipation, with every yielding to a base emotion, a person has added force to the momentum pushing him downhill. He can always, if he really wills it, break out of the mold and change his direction, but he will have to overcome the resistance of a formidable force he has arrayed against himself.

And, similarly, the capacity to do good becomes magnified with every act of goodness we have performed. An act of love strengthens our capacity to love. An act of kindness strengthens the disposition of kindness in our nature. With every good book we have read, we have enhanced our taste for good reading, and our capacity to discipline ourselves in order to pursue good reading.

We all fashion our freedom or our bondage. Our freedom to act in a certain direction grows as we exercise that freedom, and it dwindles through neglect.

Thought and Action

Thought usually precedes action, but sometimes it follows it.

In a normal situation we think before we act. The

goals sought, the costs of effort and sacrifice required to reach our goals, are all weighed. Then we proceed to effectuate what we have previously thought through.

But sometimes we work in an altogether different direction. We act before we think. We act on impulse, on a momentary whim. We act in imitation of what others do, whose example becomes contagious and carries us along to do likewise.

In many cases, it does not trouble us that we have acted without thinking. Sometimes, however, we may feel a quiet embarrassment. Our conscience may tell them that we were fools, that we betrayed our intelligence. Then we invoke a special kind of reasoning to square our conscience with the facts, and get us out of our predicament. We summon our reasoning to contrive excuses in order to justify what we have done.

A man who has been inequitable in business comforts himself by the rationalization that everybody does likewise. The man who allowed himself to quarrel or to use offensive language against another person comforts himself by arguing that the other person provoked it. He who breaks a particular practice of his religious heritage comforts himself by the rationalization that the particular practice was really old fashioned. Let a man but yield to temptation and cheat even once and he will begin to contrive excuses that morality is only a taboo, only a convention, that we live only once and must take our pleasures when we can.

Man was meant to deliberate without constraint and to be free to follow his intelligence where it leads. But intelligence itself to be trustworthy, must be free. It must not be preconditioned by an assignment to find an answer to a guilty conscience.

The Path We Have Chosen

An innate conservatism often holds us back from embarking on new adventures. Sometimes this is a brake on progress. Yet in its own way it makes a contribution to our happiness.

The world is rich in endless possibilities. Each is a path that might be pursued, that would offer many fulfillments to one who will embark on it. But if we followed the call of every possibility, we would be forever on the go. We would dissipate our strength by trying the impossible, to go in many directions at the same time, or to continue shifting from direction to direction.

Life demands that we concentrate on a given path, that we pursue it till we reach its final end. We cannot know what a given path has to offer unless we pursue it for some time, resisting the call to embark on new adventures as a diversion from the task before us.

There are times when the path we have chosen has disclosed its defects, and it becomes necessary to leave it in favor of a new path. Then it is time to abandon the promptings of a conservative disposition with its call to caution. But it is good that human nature tends to surround what we have with an aura of love, and to defend it against the disrupting pressures of a changing world.

Static and Creative Love

There are two kinds of love, the static and the creative, and both are needed in a healthy response to life.

Static love is based on the acceptance of the person as he is, with little sensitivity to his shortcomings. Sometimes the evidence of deficiency stares us in the face and we cannot ignore it. Then we apologize for it; we make allowances—as we make allowances for ourselves when we know we have done something unworthy of us.

Creative love is the longing to perfect what is ours and what is close to us. A parent's creative love for a child expresses itself in a deep concern to help him reach his highest potential, to purge him of deficiencies, to lift him beyond where he is, to where he can and, therefore, ought to be. A person loves himself creatively when he does not make allowances for his failings but struggles against the temperament or habit which causes him to fail. A static love for one's country says: My country right or wrong. It is a blind and indulgent love, which is insensitive to the true evils which prevail and subtly threaten us. A creative love is ever engaged in ferreting out our country's abuses, and seeks corrective measures that will make our country more humane—and more lovable.

But there is room in life for both loves. Indeed we need to live with both simultaneously. A static love alone would leave our world stagnant with its deficiencies. A creative love alone would make us too critical, too demanding. In the name of seeking what is better, we would alienate ourselves from what, despite its failings, still has many elements that are good. We must love those we love as they are, at the same time seeking to make them better.

Rejection and Limitation

Every act of creation, God's as well as man's, begins with a process of rejection and limitation. There were an infinite number of possible worlds in God's mind to which

He could have given birth, but He decided upon a *particular* world, imposed upon it a *particular* form, and endowed it with particular potentialities of development.

Man's creation proceeds by the same path. There were endless other forms Michelangelo could have shaped from the rock out of which he hewed his statue of Moses. All those other possibilities must have danced in his mind, and tempted him to bring them into being. But the artist banished them all, he resisted their allure, he remained consecrated to a limited vision, the vision of Moses.

How many people have injured themselves grievously because they lacked the power of rejection and limitation? They are what they are, but what they might have been continually comes back to haunt them with the reassertion of renewed claims.

While there is room in life for some rectification of wrong choices, the general demand of life is to stick to one's choice, to dismiss the enticing claims of rejected alternatives. To be *this,* one cannot be *that,* and whoever vacilates between the *this* and the *that* ends up by being a fractured person, who is pulled in many different directions, and who cannot find a sure course for his life.

A Clear Conscience

Beware of the man who lives with a clear conscience.

Dare any of us think we have loved God with all the love due Him, or, that we have loved our fellow-man with all the love due him?

Man is finite, he is fated to live by fractions. We make gestures in the right direction, toward our parents, our children, our friends, our country. But all these are only a fraction of what is called for, and they are only a fraction of what we are capable.

No matter who we are or what we are, an unused remainder of goodness remains in our being. It is a reserve on which we can draw endlessly. It is a reserve which assures us that we can attain to finer and greater levels of worth. But one needs an incentive to draw on that reserve, and the only true incentive is a discontent with things as they are.

The man with a clear conscience is smugly satisfied with himself, while a sense of guilt will make us critical and prod us endlessly to strive to be better and to do better.

When Doubt Assails the Heart

When the mind is assailed by doubt, we need to think more deeply into the issues involved. Thought is the only corrective to the shortcomings of thought.

But what if doubt assails the heart? What if we be overcome with a fear that our life may be of little worth, that the tasks we face are beyond our power to cope with, that the problems we have encountered will cause us to fail? Argument will do little to remove these doubts.

There is a therapy for the doubts of the heart—it is the momentum of life itself. If, despite our doubts, we go on living, struggling with the circumstances, drawing from within ourselves the necessary resources for meeting life's daily needs, there will occur a slow recession of doubt and a renewal of faith. A pep talk will not heal us of grief or fear.

We cannot delay life until our doubts are resolved. The resolution of our doubts often comes as a by-product of the slow immersion in the routine of living.

The Road is Long

The road is long and winding and I cannot see the end. I must proceed by slow steps, and every step I take discloses the step which comes after it. The meaning of the journey is not in the final destination, which I may or may not reach, but in the movement itself, in whatever distance I have been privileged to pass toward the far-off goal.

The patriot who strikes out for his nation's freedom cannot know the long and costly struggle it will require. He cannot know in advance how his venture will fare. His road is one episode of struggle after another, and at the conclusion of one episode, he begins to discern the outlines of the next. And the rewards of the struggle are spread out among all the episodes, each of which distills its own meaning, its own satisfaction.

A parent raising a child, a youth facing the problems and perils of the world in which he seeks to shape his destiny, the scientist seeking a cure for cancer, the reformer embarking on some cause of human amelioration —none of them possesses a blueprint for the entire road ahead. They can proceed, if at all, by concentrating on the challenge of each episode. The rewards life holds out for those who meet its commitments are not reserved for the one final moment of realization at the end, but they are apportioned on the way. Every step forward, every challenge met, every episode successfully negotiated brings with it its own reward.

The timid hold back because they cannot envision the end, but the brave proceed, trusting that the journey will become clarified as they proceed, and they are content to accept the rewards of travel, no matter when or how, or, if at all they should reach a final destination.